Italian

THE AUSTRALIAN Women's Weekly

Italian

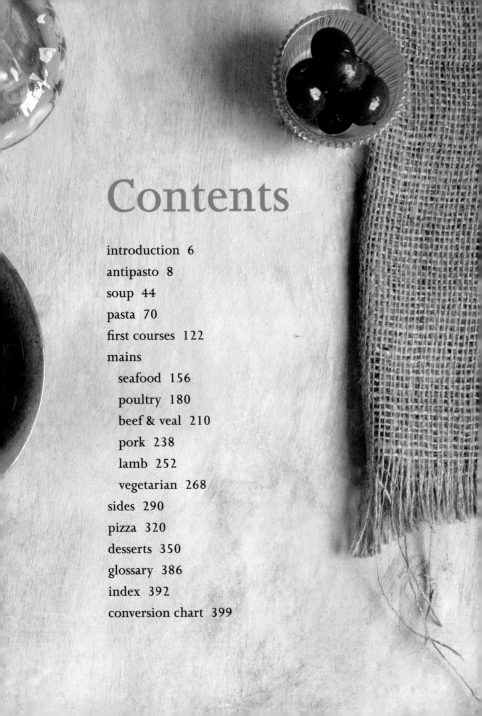

Contents

Italian food is one of the most beloved of the world's great cuisines, and it has crept into the kitchens, and certainly into the hearts, of families everywhere. The simple approach to cooking, the use of fresh seasonal produce and the deeply embedded culinary traditions of the Italians are loved around the world.

Food is an undeniable part of the Italian lifestyle, and few other cultures take as much pride in their cuisine than the Italians. Preparing and enjoying food is an extension of their lives, of their families, of their culture, and of their heritage. And it is a reflection of the way they live. Italian food is generous, sociable and always enjoyed surrounded by loved ones.

Italians cook with passion, knowledge and respect for tradition, and use only fresh seasonal produce at its best. They have perfected the art of combining simple, humble ingredients and flavours to create spectacular results.

From the peaks of the Alps to the rolling golden hills of Tuscany and the beaches of Sicily, Italy's cooking traditions reflect a wonderful regional diversity. From one region to another and even from one village to the next, cooking methods and dishes change dramatically along with what is locally produced and freshly available.

You don't have to be in Rome to do as the Romans do. Adopt their approach to cooking and eating and you will be amazed at just how effortless yet rewarding cooking Italian food is. Buon Appetito!

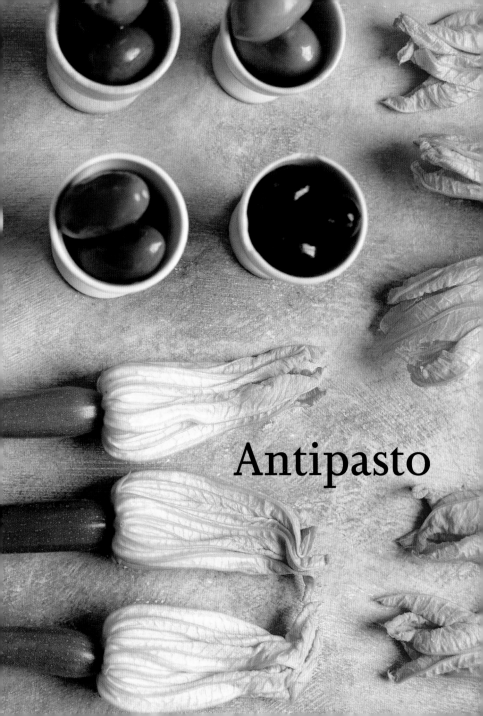

Antipasto

Roasted cherry tomato and parmesan dip

250g (8 ounces) cherry tomatoes
2 teaspoons olive oil
½ cup (120g) sour cream
½ cup (40g) finely grated parmesan cheese
2 tablespoons finely chopped fresh basil
½ teaspoon dried chilli flakes
1 stick sourdough bread (200g), sliced thinly
2 cloves garlic, halved

1 Preheat oven to 220°C/425°F.
2 Combine tomatoes and oil on oven tray. Roast, uncovered, about 15 minutes or until tomato skins split. Cool 10 minutes.
3 Combine tomatoes, sour cream, cheese, basil and chilli in medium bowl.
4 Toast bread both sides. Rub garlic onto toasts; serve with tomato and parmesan dip.

prep + cook time 35 minutes **serves** 6
nutritional count per serving 12.6g total fat (6.9g saturated fat); 932kJ (223 cal); 20g carbohydrate; 6.4g protein; 2.4g fibre

Blue cheese and caramelised onion dip

20g (¾ ounce) butter
1 large brown onion (250g), chopped coarsely
2 tablespoons brown sugar
2 tablespoons white wine vinegar
90g (3 ounces) blue cheese, crumbled
¾ cup (180g) crème fraîche
¼ cup finely chopped fresh flat-leaf parsley

1 Melt butter in medium saucepan; cook onion, stirring, until softened. Add sugar and vinegar; cook, stirring, over low heat, about 10 minutes or until onion is caramelised.
2 Stir in cheese and crème fraîche until smooth. Cool. Cover; refrigerate until cold. Stir in parsley.

prep + cook time 30 minutes **makes** 1½ cups
nutritional count per teaspoon 1.7g total fat (1.1g saturated fat); 84kJ (20 cal); 0.7g carbohydrate; 0.4g protein; 0.1g fibre

Chunky olive and herb dip

½ cup (80g) finely chopped seeded green olives
½ cup finely chopped fresh flat-leaf parsley
½ cup finely chopped fresh mint
¼ cup finely chopped fresh dill
6 drained anchovy fillets, chopped finely
2 teaspoons finely grated lemon rind
¼ cup (60ml) lemon juice
½ cup (125ml) olive oil

1 Combine ingredients in medium bowl.

prep time 20 minutes **makes** 1½ cups
nutritional count per teaspoon 1.6g total fat (0.2g saturated fat);
67kJ (16 cal); 0.3g carbohydrate; 0.1g protein; 0.1g fibre

White bean dip

1 tablespoon olive oil
1 medium leek (350g), sliced thinly
400g (13 ounces) canned white beans, rinsed, drained
1¼ cups (310ml) pouring cream
1 teaspoon finely grated lemon rind
1 tablespoon lemon juice
2 tablespoons finely chopped fresh flat-leaf parsley

1 Heat oil in small frying pan; cook leek, stirring, about 10 minutes or until leek softens. Cool.
2 Blend or process leek, beans, cream, rind and juice until smooth. Stir in parsley.

prep + cook time 25 minutes **makes** 2½ cups
nutritional count per teaspoon 1.2g total fat (0.7g saturated fat); 59kJ (14 cal); 0.4g carbohydrate; 0.2g protein; 0.2g fibre
tips You can use a 300ml carton of cream without affecting the recipe. We used cannellini beans in this recipe but you could use any white bean you like.

Fried bocconcini with roasted capsicum sauce

1 medium red capsicum (bell pepper) (200g)
2 medium egg (plum) tomatoes (150g), halved
2 cloves garlic, unpeeled
2 teaspoons olive oil
2 tablespoons plain (all-purpose) flour
1 egg, beaten lightly
½ cup (50g) packaged breadcrumbs
¼ cup (20g) finely grated parmesan cheese
2 tablespoons finely chopped fresh flat-leaf parsley
2 teaspoons finely grated lemon rind
16 cherry bocconcini cheese (240g)
vegetable oil, for deep-frying

1 Preheat oven to 220°C/425°F.
2 Quarter capsicum; remove seeds and membranes. Combine capsicum, tomato, garlic and oil in small baking dish; roast, uncovered, about 20 minutes or until vegetables soften.
3 Peel garlic; blend or process garlic and vegetable mixture until smooth.
4 Place flour and egg in separate small shallow bowls. Combine breadcrumbs, parmesan, parsley and rind in another small shallow bowl.
5 Coat bocconcini in flour; shake off excess. Dip in egg, then in breadcrumb mixture.
6 Meanwhile heat oil in wok; deep-fry bocconcini, in batches, until golden. Drain on wire rack over tray.
7 Serve bocconcini with roasted capsicum sauce.

prep + cook time 1 hour **makes** 16
nutritional count per cheese ball 4.5g total fat (2.1g saturated fat); 309kJ (74 cal); 3.8g carbohydrate; 4.3g protein; 0.5g fibre

Marinated mushrooms

1 litre (4 cups) white vinegar
1 cup (250ml) dry white wine
1 tablespoon sea salt flakes
750g (1½ pounds) button mushrooms, halved
2 cloves garlic, sliced thinly
½ teaspoon dried chilli flakes
1 tablespoon coarsely chopped fresh rosemary
1 tablespoon finely chopped fresh flat-leaf parsley
3 x 5cm (2-inch) strips lemon rind
1 bay leaf
2 cups (500ml) olive oil

1 Sterilise 1-litre (4-cup) jar and lid.
2 Heat vinegar, wine and half the salt in medium saucepan without boiling. Add mushrooms; simmer, uncovered, about 5 minutes or until tender. Drain mushrooms; discard liquid.
3 Place hot mushrooms in large heatproof bowl with garlic, chilli, herbs, rind, bay leaf and remaining salt; toss to combine. Spoon mushroom mixture into hot sterilised jar.
4 Heat oil in small saucepan; carefully pour over mushrooms in jar to completely cover mushrooms, leaving a 1cm (½ inch) space between mushrooms and top of jar. Seal while hot.

prep + cook time 40 minutes **makes** 4 cups
nutritional count per ¼ cup 28.6g total fat (4g saturated fat); 1145kJ (274 cal); 0.2g carbohydrate; 1.9g protein; 1.3g fibre
tips Store marinated mushrooms in refrigerator for up to three months. Serve mushrooms with crusty bread or as part of an antipasto platter with cheeses and deli meats.

Bruschetta

2 medium tomatoes (300g), seeded, chopped finely
½ small red onion (50g), chopped finely
1 clove garlic, crushed
1 tablespoon red wine vinegar
2 tablespoons olive oil
1 small french bread stick (150g), sliced into 2.5cm (1-inch) slices
cooking-oil spray
2 tablespoons finely shredded fresh basil

1 Preheat oven to 220°C/425°F.
2 Combine tomato, onion, garlic, vinegar and oil in small bowl.
Stand 20 minutes.
3 Meanwhile, place bread on oiled oven tray; spray with cooking oil.
Toast, in oven (or under grill), until browned both sides.
4 Stir basil into tomato mixture; spoon over toast.

prep + cook time 15 minutes (+ standing) **makes** 12
nutritional count per bruschetta 4.3g total fat (0.5g saturated fat);
318kJ (76 cal); 7.4g carbohydrate; 1.5g protein; 0.9g fibre

Giardiniera (pickled vegetables)

2 medium red capsicums (bell pepper) (400g)
1 litre (4 cups) white vinegar
2 cups (500ml) water
6 black peppercorns
1 bay leaf
1 tablespoon sea salt flakes
1 small eggplant (230g), quartered lengthways,
   cut into 1cm (½-inch) slices
½ small cauliflower (200g), cut into florets
2 medium carrots (240g), sliced thinly diagonally
2 stalks celery (300g), trimmed, sliced thickly on the diagonal
2 tablespoons finely chopped fresh flat-leaf parsley
2 teaspoons finely chopped fresh thyme
2 cups (500ml) olive oil
2 cloves garlic, sliced thinly

1 Preheat oven to 200°C/400°F. Sterilise 1.5-litre (6-cup) jar and lid.
2 Quarter capsicums; discard seeds and membranes. Roast capsicum, skin-side up, until skin blisters and blackens. Cover capsicum with plastic wrap or paper for 5 minutes; peel away skin then slice thickly.
3 Meanwhile, combine vinegar, the water, peppercorns, bay leaf and half the salt in large saucepan; heat without boiling. Add eggplant, cauliflower, carrot and celery; bring to the boil. Reduce heat; simmer, uncovered, about 5 minutes or until vegetables are tender. Drain vegetables; discard liquid.
4 Combine hot vegetables, capsicum, herbs and remaining salt in large heatproof bowl. Spoon vegetable mixture into sterilised jar.
5 Heat oil and garlic in small saucepan, strain into large heatproof jug; discard garlic. Carefully pour hot oil over vegetables in jar to completely cover vegetables, leaving a 1cm (½-inch) space between vegetables and top of jar. Seal while hot.

prep + cook time 1 hour **makes** 6 cups
nutritional count per ¼ cup 19.1g total fat (2.7g saturated fat); 748kJ (179 cal); 1.6g carbohydrate; 0.7g protein; 1g fibre
tip Store in the refrigerator for up to three months.

Frittata with two toppings

2 tablespoons extra virgin olive oil
1 medium brown onion (150g), chopped finely
2 tablespoons coarsely chopped fresh flat-leaf parsley
2 tablespoons finely grated parmesan cheese
10 eggs, beaten lightly
20g (¾ ounce) butter
2 cloves garlic, crushed
8 button mushrooms
4 char-grilled artichokes, halved
¼ cup (50g) char-grilled red capsicum (bell pepper), sliced thinly

1 Heat oil in medium frying pan; cook onion, stirring, until soft.
Stir in half the parsley. Add cheese and eggs to pan; cook over
low heat, covered loosely, about 8 minutes or until edges are set.
2 Preheat grill (broiler).
3 Place pan under hot grill (shielding handle with foil, if necessary)
until browned lightly and just set. Invert onto cutting board.
4 Meanwhile, heat butter in small frying pan; cook garlic and mushrooms,
stirring, until just tender; stir in remaining parsley.
5 Cut frittata into 16 wedges, arrange on a serving platter. Top half the
wedges with the mushrooms and half with artichokes and capsicum.

prep + cook time 30 minutes **serves** 8
nutritional count per serving 14.4g total fat (4.4g saturated fat);
732kJ (175 cal); 1.5g carbohydrate; 10g protein; 0.7g fibre

Warm olives with garlic, chilli and oregano

¾ cup (180ml) extra virgin olive oil
1 fresh long red chilli, sliced thinly
1 clove garlic, sliced thinly
¼ cup coarsely chopped fresh oregano leaves
500g (1 pound) black and green olives

1 Gently heat oil in large frying pan, add chilli, garlic and oregano; stir until warm and fragrant.
2 Add olives; shake the pan until warmed through.
3 Serve olives with grissini, if you like.

prep + cook time 10 minutes **serves** 8
nutritional count per serving 21.2g total fat (3g saturated fat); 1037kJ (248 cal); 14.1g carbohydrate; 0.5g protein; 0.8g fibre

Melon in prosciutto

1 small rockmelon (1.3kg), halved lengthways
12 thin slices prosciutto (180g)
2 tablespoons extra virgin olive oil
¼ cup loosely packed fresh flat-leaf parsley leaves

1 Peel and seed rockmelon; cut into 12 wedges.
2 Wrap one prosciutto slice around each melon wedge, place on serving platter; drizzle with oil, sprinkle with parsley.

prep time 20 minutes **serves** 4
nutritional count per serving 11.9g total fat (2.2g saturated fat); 802kJ (192 cal); 10.9g carbohydrate; 9.4g protein; 2.5g fibre

Parmesan scones with goat's cheese and tapenade

1½ cups (225g) self-raising flour
30g (1 ounce) butter
¼ cup (30g) finely grated parmesan cheese
¾ cup (180ml) buttermilk, approximately
180g (6 ounces) goat's cheese
bunch fresh flat-leaf parsley

tapenade
200g (6½ ounces) seeded black olives
1 tablespoon rinsed drained capers
1 clove garlic, quartered
½ cup coarsely chopped fresh flat-leaf parsley
5 drained anchovy fillets
1 tablespoon lemon juice
1 tablespoon olive oil

1 Preheat oven to 200°C/400°F. Oil oven tray.
2 Sift flour into large bowl; rub in butter, then stir in parmesan. Using a knife, mix in enough buttermilk to make a soft dough.
3 Turn dough onto floured surface, knead lightly until smooth. Press dough out to 1.5cm (½-inch) thickness, cut out 30 x 3cm (1-inch) rounds. Place scones, barely touching each other, on tray.
4 Bake scones about 20 minutes. Turn onto wire rack; cover, cool.
5 Meanwhile, make tapenade.
6 Split scones in half, top each half with tapenade and goat's cheese; top each with a parsley leaf.
tapenade Process ingredients until chopped coarsely.

prep + cook time 45 minutes **makes** 60
nutritional count per scone 9.2g total fat (4.8g saturated fat); 849kJ (203 cal); 21.9g carbohydrate; 7.4g protein; 1.5g fibre
tip Good quality tapenade is easy to buy if you don't want to make your own.

Mini baked herb ricotta

250g (8 ounces) ricotta cheese
1 egg
1 tablespoon finely chopped fresh flat-leaf parsley
1 teaspoon finely chopped fresh thyme
1 clove garlic, crushed

1 Preheat oven to 180°C/350°F. Oil 18 holes of two 12-hole
(1½-tablespoon/20ml) mini muffin pans.
2 Blend or process ingredients until smooth. Spoon mixture into pan holes.
3 Bake ricotta about 20 minutes or until browned lightly.

prep + cook time 30 minutes **makes** 18
nutritional count per ricotta 1.9g total fat (1.1g saturated fat);
105kJ (25 cal); 0.2g carbohydrate; 1.8g protein; 0g fibre

Arancini

2 cups (500ml) chicken stock
½ cup (125ml) dry white wine
45g (1½ ounces) butter
1 small brown onion (80g), chopped finely
1 clove garlic, crushed
1 cup (200g) arborio rice
⅓ cup (25g) finely grated parmesan cheese
⅓ cup (35g) coarsely grated mozzarella cheese
24 fetta-stuffed green olives (240g)
⅓ cup (35g) packaged breadcrumbs
vegetable oil, for deep-frying

1 Combine stock and wine in medium saucepan; bring to the boil. Reduce heat; simmer, covered.
2 Meanwhile, melt butter in medium saucepan; cook onion and garlic, stirring, until onion softens. Add rice; stir over medium heat until rice is coated in butter mixture. Stir in ½ cup of the simmering stock mixture; cook, stirring, over low heat until liquid is absorbed. Continue adding mixture, in ½ cup batches, stirring, until liquid is absorbed after each addition. Total cooking time should be about 35 minutes or until rice is tender. Stir in cheeses, cover; cool 30 minutes.
3 Roll rounded tablespoons of risotto mixture into balls; press an olive into centre of each ball, roll to enclose. Coat risotto balls in breadcrumbs.
4 Heat oil in wok; deep-fry risotto balls, in batches, until browned lightly. Drain on absorbent paper.

prep + cook time 1 hour 30 minutes (+ cooling) **makes** 24
nutritional count per arancini 5.7g total fat (1.8g saturated fat); 401kJ (96 cal); 8.1g carbohydrate; 1.9g protein; 1g fibre

Eggplant fritters

2 large eggplants (1kg)
1 cup (100g) coarsely grated mozzarella cheese
½ cup coarsely chopped fresh flat-leaf parsley
2 cloves garlic, crushed
½ cup (50g) packaged breadcrumbs
¼ cup (35g) plain (all-purpose) flour
2 eggs
vegetable oil, for shallow-frying

1 Preheat oven to 220°C/425°F.
2 Remove and discard stem ends from eggplants; prick eggplants all over with fork. Place on oiled oven tray; roast, uncovered, about 30 minutes or until soft. Cool. Peel eggplants; chop flesh finely.
3 Combine eggplant, cheese, parsley, garlic, breadcrumbs, flour and eggs in large bowl. Using wetted hands, shape level tablespoons of mixture into oval patties.
4 Heat oil in large frying pan; cook fritters, in batches, until browned both sides. Drain on absorbent paper. Serve with lemon wedges, if you like.

prep + cook time 1 hour **makes** 36
nutritional count per fritter 5.3g total fat (1g saturated fat); 272kJ (65 cal); 2.4g carbohydrate; 1.7g protein; 0.8g fibre

Artichoke and asparagus fritters with olive relish

185g (6 ounces) asparagus, trimmed, chopped finely
280g (9 ounces) jar artichokes in brine, drained, chopped finely
2 eggs
2 tablespoons finely chopped fresh mint
½ cup (40g) finely grated parmesan cheese
¼ cup (35g) self-raising flour
vegetable oil, for shallow frying
olive relish
½ cup (60g) seeded green olives, chopped finely
½ cup (60g) seeded black olives, chopped finely
¼ cup finely chopped fresh flat-leaf parsley
1 tablespoon finely chopped fresh chives
1 tablespoon olive oil
1 tablespoon lemon juice

1 Make olive relish.
2 Combine asparagus, artichoke, eggs, mint, cheese and flour in medium bowl.
3 Heat oil in large frying pan; shallow-fry heaped tablespoons of mixture, in batches, until browned all over and cooked through. Drain on absorbent paper. Serve hot with relish.
olive relish Combine ingredients in small bowl.

prep + cook time 40 minutes **makes** 15
nutritional count per fritter 4.6g total fat (1.2g saturated fat); 288kJ (69 cal); 3.8g carbohydrate; 2.9g protein; 0.8g fibre

Cod and olive fritters

625g (1¼ pounds) salted cod fillet, skin on
3 medium potatoes (600g), halved
1 tablespoon olive oil
1 medium brown onion (150g), chopped finely
2 cloves garlic, crushed
¼ cup finely chopped fresh flat-leaf parsley
½ cup (60g) seeded green olives, chopped finely
1 egg
vegetable oil, for deep-frying

1 Rinse fish under cold water to remove excess salt. Place fish in large bowl, cover with cold water; refrigerate, covered, overnight, changing the water three or four times. Drain fish; discard water.
2 Place fish in large saucepan, cover with cold water; bring to the boil uncovered. Reduce heat, simmer, covered, 5 minutes. Drain fish, discard water; remove skin and bones then flake fish.
3 Boil, steam or microwave potato until tender; drain. Roughly mash potato in large bowl.
4 Meanwhile, heat olive oil in large frying pan; cook onion and garlic, stirring, until onion softens.
5 Combine fish, onion mixture, parsley, olives and egg with potato; mix well.
6 Roll level tablespoons of fish mixture into balls, place on baking-paper-lined tray; refrigerate 30 minutes.
7 Heat vegetable oil in deep medium saucepan; deep-fry fritters, in batches, until browned and heated through. Drain on absorbent paper.

prep + cook time 1 hour 30 minutes (+ refrigeration) **makes** 40
nutritional count per fritter 2.6g total fat (0.4g saturated fat);
196kJ (47 cal); 47.4g carbohydrate; 3.6g protein; 0.3g fibre
tip Salted cod, also known as salt cod, baccalà, bacalhau, bacalao and morue, is available from Italian, Spanish and Portuguese delicatessens and some specialty food stores. It needs to be de-salted and rehydrated before use.

Soup

Minestrone

1 ham hock (1kg)
1 medium brown onion (150g),
  quartered
1 stalk celery (150g), trimmed,
  chopped coarsely
1 teaspoon black peppercorns
1 bay leaf
4 litres (16 cups) water
1 tablespoon olive oil
1 large carrot (180g),
  chopped finely
2 stalks celery (300g), trimmed,
  chopped finely, extra
3 cloves garlic, crushed

¼ cup (70g) tomato paste
2 large tomatoes (440g),
  chopped finely
1 small leek (200g), sliced thinly
1 cup (100g) small pasta shells
410g (13 ounces) canned
  white beans, rinsed, drained
½ cup coarsely chopped
  fresh flat-leaf parsley
½ cup coarsely chopped
  fresh basil
½ cup (40g) flaked parmesan
  cheese

1 Preheat oven to 220°C/425°F.
2 Roast ham hock and onion in baking dish, uncovered, 30 minutes.
3 Place hock and onion in large saucepan with celery, peppercorns,
bay leaf and the water; bring to the boil. Reduce heat; simmer,
uncovered, 2 hours.
4 Remove hock from broth. Strain broth through muslin-lined sieve or
colander into large heatproof bowl; discard solids. Allow broth to cool;
cover, refrigerate until cold.
5 Remove ham from hock; shred coarsely. Discard bone, fat and skin.
6 Meanwhile, heat oil in large saucepan; cook carrot and extra celery,
stirring, 2 minutes. Add shredded ham, garlic, paste and tomato; cook,
stirring, 2 minutes.
7 Discard fat from surface of broth. Pour broth into a large measuring
jug; add enough water to make 2 litres (8 cups). Add broth to pan;
bring to the boil. Reduce heat; simmer, covered, 20 minutes.
8 Add leek, pasta and beans to pan; bring to the boil. Reduce heat;
simmer, uncovered, until pasta is tender. Remove from heat; stir in herbs.
Serve soup sprinkled with cheese.

prep + cook time 4 hours (+ refrigeration) **serves** 6
nutritional count per serving 7.2g total fat (2.4g saturated fat);
865kJ (207 cal); 19.6g carbohydrate; 12.7g protein; 6.1g fibre

Tuscan bean soup

2 tablespoons olive oil
3 medium brown onions (450g), chopped coarsely
2 cloves garlic, crushed
200g (6½-ounce) piece speck, bacon or pancetta,
    chopped coarsely
2 medium carrots (240g), chopped coarsely
2 stalks celery (300g), trimmed, chopped coarsely
800g (1½ pounds) canned diced tomatoes
¼ medium savoy cabbage (375g), shredded coarsely
1 medium zucchini (120g), chopped coarsely
2 sprigs fresh thyme
2 cups (500ml) beef stock
2 litres (8 cups) water
400g (13 ounces) canned borlotti beans, rinsed, drained
6 thick slices ciabatta bread

1 Heat oil in large saucepan; cook onion, garlic and speck, stirring,
about 5 minutes or until onion is soft.
2 Add carrot, celery, undrained tomatoes, cabbage, zucchini, thyme, stock
and the water; bring to the boil. Reduce heat; simmer, uncovered, 2 hours.
3 Add beans; simmer, uncovered, 20 minutes.
4 Meanwhile, preheat grill (broiler); toast bread. Place a slice of bread
in the base of each serving bowl, top with soup. Drizzle with a little extra
olive oil, if you like.

prep + cook time 2 hours 45 minutes **serves** 6
nutritional count per serving 11.8g total fat (2.7g saturated fat);
1133kJ (271 cal); 22.9g carbohydrate; 14.1g protein; 8.3g fibre

Seafood soup with gremolata

2kg (4 pounds) fish bones
1 medium brown onion (150g),
 chopped coarsely
1 medium carrot (120g),
 chopped coarsely
2 stalks celery (300g), trimmed,
 chopped coarsely
4 litres (16 cups) water
8 black peppercorns
2 bay leaves
1 tablespoon olive oil
1 medium brown onion (150g),
 chopped coarsely, extra
2 cloves garlic, crushed
5 medium tomatoes (950g),
 chopped coarsely

3 teaspoons sugar
400g (13 ounces) canned
 tomatoes
¼ cup (60g) tomato paste
½ cup (125ml) dry white wine
2 uncooked medium lobster tails
 (760g), shelled, chopped coarsely
410g (13 ounces) boneless
 firm white fish fillets,
 chopped coarsely

gremolata
1 clove garlic, chopped finely
1 tablespoon finely chopped
 lemon rind
2 tablespoons finely chopped
 fresh flat-leaf parsley

1 Combine fish bones, onion, carrot, celery, the water, peppercorns and bay leaves in large saucepan. Simmer, uncovered, 20 minutes. Strain stock over large bowl; discard bones and vegetables.
2 Heat oil in large saucepan; cook extra onion and garlic, stirring, until onion softens. Add fresh tomato and sugar; cook, stirring, 10 minutes or until tomato is soft. Stir in undrained crushed tomatoes, paste and wine; bring to the boil. Reduce heat; simmer, uncovered, about 5 minutes or until mixture has thickened slightly, stirring occasionally. Add stock, bring to the boil; simmer, uncovered, 20 minutes. Cool 10 minutes.
3 Blend or process tomato mixture, in batches, until smooth; return to same cleaned pan, bring to the boil. Add lobster and fish; simmer, stirring, about 5 minutes or until seafood is just cooked.
4 Meanwhile, make gremolata.
5 Divide soup among serving bowls; sprinkle each with gremolata.
gremolata Combine ingredients in small bowl.

prep + cook time 1 hour 50 minutes (+ cooling) **serves** 6
nutritional count per serving 13.2g total fat (3.5g saturated fat); 2629kJ (629 cal); 12.4g carbohydrate; 108g protein; 5g fibre

Stracciatella

5 eggs
½ cup finely grated parmesan cheese
1.5 litres (6 cups) chicken stock
2 tablespoons finely chopped fresh flat-leaf parsley
pinch of nutmeg

1 Lightly whisk eggs with cheese in medium jug until combined.
2 Bring stock to the boil in large saucepan. Remove pan from heat; gradually add egg mixture, whisking constantly.
3 Return pan to heat; simmer, stirring constantly, about 5 minutes or until egg mixture forms fine shreds. Stir in parsley and nutmeg.

prep + cook time 15 minutes **serves** 6
nutritional count per serving 7.6g total fat (3.2g saturated fat); 493kJ (118 cal); 1.9g carbohydrate; 10.9g protein; 0.1g fibre

Chicken and risoni soup with herbed meatballs

2.5 litres (10 cups) water
1.6kg (3¼ pounds) whole chicken
1 large tomato (220g), halved
2 stalks celery (300g),
  trimmed, halved
1 medium brown onion (150g),
  halved
2 fresh flat-leaf parsley stalks
5 black peppercorns
280g (9 ounces) minced (ground)
  chicken
½ cup (50g) packaged
  breadcrumbs

2 tablespoons finely chopped
  fresh flat-leaf parsley
2 tablespoons finely grated
  parmesan cheese
1 egg
1 tablespoon olive oil
¾ cup (165g) risoni
2 tablespoons lemon juice
⅓ cup coarsely chopped fresh
  flat-leaf parsley

1 Place the water in large saucepan with whole chicken, tomato, celery, onion, parsley stalks and peppercorns; bring to the boil. Reduce heat; simmer, covered, 2 hours.

2 Remove chicken from pan. Strain broth through muslin-lined sieve or colander into large heatproof bowl; discard solids. Allow broth to cool, cover; refrigerate overnight. When chicken is cool enough to handle, remove and discard skin and bones. Shred meat coarsely; cover, refrigerate overnight.

3 Combine mince, breadcrumbs, finely chopped parsley, cheese and egg in medium bowl; roll rounded teaspoons of mixture into balls. Heat oil in medium saucepan; cook meatballs, in batches, until browned all over.

4 Skim and discard fat from surface of broth. Return broth to large saucepan; bring to the boil. Reduce heat; simmer, uncovered, 20 minutes. Add meatballs and pasta; simmer, uncovered, about 10 minutes or until meatballs are cooked through and pasta is just tender. Add 2 cups of the reserved chicken (keep remaining chicken for another use), juice and coarsely chopped parsley to pan; stir soup over medium heat until hot.

prep + cook time 3 hours 15 minutes (+ refrigeration) **serves** 4
nutritional count per serving 45.8g total fat (3.7g saturated fat); 3536kJ (846 cal); 40.4g carbohydrate; 66.3g protein; 4.3g fibre

Creamy semi-dried tomato and veal soup

500g (1-pound) piece boneless veal shoulder
1 litre (4 cups) water
6 black peppercorns
1 bay leaf
60g (2 ounces) butter
1 medium brown onion (150g), chopped coarsely
1 clove garlic, crushed
⅓ cup (50g) plain (all-purpose) flour
6 large egg (plum) tomatoes (540g), chopped coarsely
2 tablespoons tomato paste
½ cup (125ml) pouring cream
⅓ cup (75g) semi-dried tomatoes, drained, chopped finely
2 tablespoons finely shredded fresh basil

1 Place veal and the water in large saucepan with peppercorns and bay leaf; bring to the boil. Reduce heat; simmer, covered, about 1 ½ hours or until veal is tender.
2 Transfer veal to medium bowl; using two forks, shred veal coarsely. Strain broth through muslin-lined sieve or colander into large heatproof bowl; discard solids.
3 Melt butter in large saucepan; cook onion and garlic, stirring, until onion softens. Add flour; cook, stirring, until mixture thickens and bubbles. Gradually stir in broth; stir over medium heat until soup boils and thickens slightly. Add egg tomato and paste; return to the boil. Reduce heat; simmer, covered, 10 minutes. Cool 15 minutes.
4 Blend or process soup, in batches, until smooth. Return soup to same cleaned pan, add cream; stir over medium heat until hot.
5 Serve bowls of soup topped with shredded veal and semi-dried tomato, sprinkled with basil. If you like, accompany soup with toasted ciabatta and herb butter.

prep + cook time 2 hours 30 minutes (+ cooling) **serves** 6
nutritional count per serving 20.1g total fat (12g saturated fat); 1430kJ (342 cal); 15.3g carbohydrate; 23.2g protein; 4.2g fibre

Roasted capsicum soup with fried provolone polenta

4 medium red capsicums
(bell peppers) (800g)
2 cloves garlic, unpeeled
1 tablespoon olive oil
1 medium brown onion (150g),
chopped finely
1 teaspoon sweet paprika
3 cups (750ml) water
1 litre (4 cups) chicken stock
½ cup (125ml) pouring cream

2 teaspoons white sugar
1 tablespoon finely chopped
fresh chives
provolone polenta
3½ cups (875ml) water
1 cup (170g) polenta
20g (¾ ounce) butter
1 cup coarsely grated
provolone cheese

1 Three hours before, make provolone polenta.

2 Quarter capsicums, discard seeds and membranes. Roast capsicum and garlic under grill or in very hot oven, skin-side up, until skin blisters and blackens. Cover capsicum pieces in plastic or paper for 5 minutes, peel away skin. Peel garlic; chop coarsely.

3 Heat oil in large saucepan; cook onion, stirring, until softened. Add paprika; cook, stirring, until fragrant.

4 Add the water, stock, capsicum and garlic; bring to the boil. Reduce heat; simmer, uncovered, 40 minutes. Cool 15 minutes.

5 Meanwhile, turn polenta onto board, trim edges; cut in half lengthways, cut each half into 9 finger-sized slices. Cook polenta, in batches, in heated oiled large frying pan until browned both sides.

6 Blend or process soup, in batches, until smooth. Return soup to same cleaned pan, add cream and sugar; stir over medium heat until hot.

7 Serve soup sprinkled with chives, accompanied with fried polenta.

provolone polenta Oil 20cm x 30cm (8-inch x 12-inch) lamington pan; line base and long sides with baking paper, extending paper 5cm (2 inches) over long sides. Bring the water to the boil in medium saucepan. Gradually add polenta, stirring constantly. Reduce heat; simmer, stirring, about 10 minutes or until polenta thickens. Stir in butter and cheese. Spread polenta into pan, cover; refrigerate about 3 hours or until firm.

prep + cook time 1 hour 30 minutes (+ cooling & refrigeration) **serves** 6
nutritional count per serving (incl. polenta) 21.6g total fat (12g saturated fat); 1484kJ (355 cal); 27.3g carbohydrate; 11.7g protein; 3.3g fibre

Spicy tomato soup with ricotta ravioli and rocket pesto

⅓ cup (80g) ricotta cheese
2 tablespoons finely grated
  parmesan cheese
2 fresh lasagne sheets (100g)
1 egg, beaten lightly
1 tablespoon olive oil
1 large onion (200g), chopped
1 clove garlic, crushed
1 fresh small red thai chilli,
  chopped finely
750g (1½ pounds) egg (plum)
  tomatoes, seeded, chopped
2 stalks celery (300g), trimmed,
  chopped coarsely

2 cups (500ml) vegetable stock
410g (13 ounces) canned
  tomato puree
rocket pesto
20g baby rocket (arugula) leaves
¼ cup (35g) roasted unsalted
  pistachios
¼ cup (20g) coarsely grated
  parmesan cheese
1 clove garlic, quartered
2 tablespoons olive oil
1 tablespoon lemon juice
1 tablespoon water

1 Combine cheeses in small bowl. Cut each lasagne sheet into 24 squares. Place level half-teaspoons of cheese mixture in centre of 24 squares, brush edges with egg; top with remaining squares, press around edges to seal. Place ravioli, in single layer, on tray, cover; refrigerate 20 minutes.
2 Meanwhile, heat oil in large saucepan; cook onion, garlic and chilli, stirring, until onion softens. Add chopped tomato, celery and stock; bring to the boil. Reduce heat; simmer, covered, 20 minutes or until celery is tender. Cool 15 minutes.
3 Make rocket pesto.
4 Blend or process soup, in batches, until smooth. Return soup to same cleaned pan, add tomato puree; bring to the boil. Reduce heat; simmer, uncovered, 10 minutes.
5 Meanwhile, cook ravioli, uncovered, in large saucepan of boiling salted water until they float to the surface; drain then stir into soup.
6 Serve bowls of soup, with ravioli, topped with pesto.
rocket pesto Blend or process rocket, nuts, cheese and garlic until chopped coarsely. With motor operating, gradually add oil; process until mixture forms a thick paste. Stir in juice and water.

prep + cook time 1 hour 20 minutes (+ refrigeration & cooling) **serves** 4
nutritional count per serving 25.1g total fat (6.1g saturated fat);
1814kJ (434 cal); 32.6g carbohydrate; 15.8g protein; 8.2g fibre

Cream of mushroom and pancetta soup

15g (½ ounce) dried porcini mushrooms
1 cup (250ml) boiling water
45g (1½ ounces) butter
1 medium brown onion (150g), chopped coarsely
1 small leek (200g), sliced thinly
250g (8 ounces) button mushrooms, sliced thickly
⅓ cup (80ml) dry white wine
3 cups (750ml) chicken stock
1 large potato (300g), chopped coarsely
1¼ cups (310ml) pouring cream
2 tablespoons coarsely chopped fresh tarragon
6 slices pancetta (90g)

1 Place porcini mushrooms and the water in small heatproof bowl; stand 30 minutes. Drain through fine sieve into small bowl; reserve liquid. Chop porcini coarsely.
2 Meanwhile, melt butter in large saucepan; cook onion and leek, stirring, until vegetables soften. Add button mushrooms; cook, stirring, about 10 minutes or until mushrooms soften and liquid evaporates. Add wine; cook, stirring, about 5 minutes or until liquid reduces by half. Add reserved porcini liquid, stock and potato; bring to the boil. Reduce heat; simmer, uncovered, about 10 minutes or until potato is tender. Remove soup from heat; cool 15 minutes.
3 Blend or process soup, in batches, until smooth, return to same cleaned pan; bring to the boil. Add cream; reduce heat, stir over medium heat until soup is hot. Remove from heat; stir in tarragon.
4 Meanwhile, cook pancetta in heated medium frying pan until crisp; drain on absorbent paper.
5 Serve bowls of soup sprinkled with porcini and crumbled pancetta.

prep + cook time 1 hour 10 minutes (+ standing & cooling) **serves** 4
nutritional count per serving 44.9g total fat (28.4g saturated fat); 2228kJ (533 cal); 15.6g carbohydrate; 13g protein; 4g fibre
tip You can use a 300ml carton of cream without affecting the recipe.

Cream of roasted garlic and potato soup

2 medium garlic bulbs (140g), unpeeled
2 tablespoons olive oil
2 medium brown onions (300g), chopped coarsely
1 tablespoon fresh thyme leaves
5 medium potatoes (1kg), chopped coarsely
1.25 litres (5 cups) chicken stock
¾ cup (180ml) pouring cream

1 Preheat oven to 180°C/350°F.
2 Separate garlic bulbs into cloves; place unpeeled cloves, in single layer, on oven tray. Drizzle with half the oil. Roast about 15 minutes or until garlic is soft. Remove from oven; when cool enough to handle, squeeze garlic into small bowl, discard skins.
3 Meanwhile, heat remaining oil in large saucepan; cook onion and thyme, stirring, until onion softens. Add potato; cook, stirring, 5 minutes. Add stock; bring to the boil. Reduce heat; simmer, uncovered, about 15 minutes or until potato is just tender. Stir in garlic; simmer, uncovered, 5 minutes. Cool 10 minutes.
4 Blend or process soup, in batches, until smooth. Return soup to same cleaned pan; stir over heat until hot, then stir in cream.
5 Divide soup among serving bowls; sprinkle with extra thyme, if you like.

prep + cook time 40 minutes (+ cooling) **serves** 4
nutritional count per serving 27.9g total fat (13g saturated fat); 1864kJ (446 cal); 36.8g carbohydrate; 12g protein; 8.5g fibre

Lentil soup

1 tablespoon olive oil
3 rindless bacon slices (195g), chopped coarsely
1 medium brown onion (150g), chopped finely
1 medium carrot (120g), chopped finely
1 stalk celery (150g), trimmed, chopped finely
1 cup (200g) brown lentils
410g (13 ounces) canned crushed tomatoes
1 litre (4 cups) chicken stock
1 bay leaf
¼ cup coarsely chopped fresh flat-leaf parsley

1 Heat oil in large saucepan; cook bacon, onion, carrot and celery, stirring, until onion softens.
2 Add lentils, undrained tomatoes, stock and bay leaf; bring to the boil. Reduce heat; simmer, covered, 30 minutes.
3 Discard bay leaf; serve soup sprinkled with parsley.

prep + cook time 1 hour **serves** 4
nutritional count per serving 13.4g total fat (3.7g saturated fat); 1484kJ (355 cal); 27.8g carbohydrate; 26.1g protein; 10.1g fibre

Creamy chickpea and garlic soup

2 cups (400g) dried chickpeas (garbanzo)
1 tablespoon olive oil
1 large brown onion (200g), chopped coarsely
4 cloves garlic, crushed
1.75 litres (7 cups) water
2 bay leaves
1 sprig fresh rosemary
1¼ cups (310ml) pouring cream

1 Place chickpeas in large bowl, cover with water; stand overnight, drain. Rinse under cold water, drain.
2 Heat oil in large saucepan; cook onion and garlic, stirring, until onion softens. Add chickpeas, the water, bay leaves and rosemary; bring to the boil. Reduce heat; simmer, covered, about 2 hours or until chickpeas are tender. Remove from heat; cool 5 minutes.
3 Discard bay leaves and rosemary. Using hand-held blender, process soup in pan until smooth. Add cream; stir over medium heat until hot.

prep + cook time 2 hours 30 minutes (+ standing) **serves** 4
nutritional count per serving 39.9g total fat (22.5g saturated fat); 2048kJ (490 cal); 21.1g carbohydrate; 10g protein; 6.9g fibre
tip You can use a 300ml carton of cream without affecting the recipe.

Pasta

Fettuccine carbonara

500g (1 pound) fresh fettuccine pasta
60g (2 ounces) butter
6 rindless bacon slices (390g), sliced thinly
1 clove garlic, crushed
½ teaspoon cracked black pepper
1¼ cups (310ml) pouring cream
2 eggs, beaten lightly
½ cup (40g) finely grated parmesan cheese
½ cup (40g) finely grated romano cheese
2 teaspoons coarsely chopped fresh chives

1 Cook pasta in large saucepan of boiling water until tender; drain.
2 Meanwhile, melt butter in medium frying pan; cook bacon, stirring, about 5 minutes.
3 Add garlic, pepper and cream to pan; simmer, uncovered, until sauce reduces by half. Remove from heat. Stir in egg and cheeses.
4 Add pasta to sauce; stir to coat. Serve pasta sprinkled with chives.

prep + cook time 30 minutes **serves** 4
nutritional count per serving 66.7g total fat (39g saturated fat); 3662kJ (876 cal); 33.6g carbohydrate; 53.7g protein; 2.4g fibre
tip You can use a 300ml carton of cream without affecting the recipe.

Mushroom fettuccine boscaiola

15g (½ ounce) dried porcini mushrooms
¼ cup (60ml) boiling water
375g (12 ounces) fettuccine pasta
1 tablespoon olive oil
200g (6½ ounces) pancetta, chopped coarsely
90g (3 ounces) button mushrooms, sliced thinly
90g (3 ounces) swiss brown mushrooms, sliced thinly
1 flat mushroom (80g), sliced thinly
2 cloves garlic, crushed
¼ cup (60ml) dry white wine
1¼ cups (310ml) pouring cream
1 tablespoon lemon juice
½ cup (40g) finely grated parmesan cheese
2 tablespoons coarsely chopped fresh chives
2 tablespoons finely grated parmesan cheese, extra

1 Combine porcini mushrooms and the water in small heatproof bowl; cover, stand 15 minutes or until mushrooms are tender. Drain; reserve soaking liquid, chop mushrooms coarsely.
2 Cook pasta in large saucepan of boiling water until tender; drain.
3 Meanwhile, heat oil in large frying pan; cook pancetta until crisp. Add all mushrooms and garlic; cook, stirring, until mushrooms are browned lightly. Add wine; bring to the boil. Boil, uncovered, until liquid has almost evaporated. Add cream, juice and reserved soaking liquid; simmer, uncovered, until sauce reduces by half and thickens slightly. Stir in cheese and chives.
4 Combine pasta and sauce in large bowl. Serve pasta sprinkled with extra cheese.

prep + cook time 40 minutes (+ standing) **serves** 4
nutritional count per serving 45.5g total fat (26.1g saturated fat); 3390kJ (811 cal); 66.9g carbohydrate; 28.9g protein; 5.3g fibre
tip You can use a 300ml carton of cream without affecting the recipe.

Fettuccine marinara

500g (1 pound) fresh fettuccine pasta
1 tablespoon olive oil
1 small brown onion (80g), chopped finely
2 tablespoons tomato paste
½ cup (125ml) dry white wine
3 cups (750ml) bottled tomato pasta sauce
750g (1½ pounds) marinara mix
pinch saffron threads

1 Cook pasta in large saucepan of boiling water until tender; drain.
2 Heat oil in large saucepan; cook onion, stirring, until soft. Add paste; cook, stirring, 1 minute. Add wine; bring to the boil. Reduce heat; simmer, uncovered, 3 minutes.
3 Add sauce, marinara mix and saffron; bring to the boil. Reduce heat; simmer, uncovered, about 5 minutes or until seafood is cooked through. Serve pasta topped with sauce.

prep + cook time 45 minutes serves 4
nutritional count per serving 12.1g total fat (2.5g saturated fat); 3490kJ (835 cal); 104.3g carbohydrate; 66g protein; 7.9g fibre

Tagliatelle with grilled vegetables and basil tapenade

1 large eggplant (500g), sliced thickly
2 large zucchini (300g), sliced thickly
250g (8 ounces) cherry tomatoes
375g (12 ounces) tagliatelle pasta
1 cup loosely packed fresh basil leaves
basil tapenade
2½ cups (300g) seeded black olives
2 tablespoons drained capers, rinsed
1 clove garlic, quartered
2 tablespoons lemon juice
¼ cup loosely packed fresh basil leaves
⅓ cup (80ml) olive oil

1 Make basil tapenade.
2 Cook eggplant, zucchini and tomatoes, in batches, on heated oiled grill plate (or grill or grill pan) until browned.
3 Meanwhile, cook pasta in large saucepan of boiling water, uncovered, until just tender; drain.
4 Place pasta in medium bowl with vegetables, tapenade and basil; toss gently to combine.
basil tapenade Blend or process ingredients until smooth.

prep + cook time 45 minutes **serves** 4
nutritional count per serving 20.7g total fat (2.9g saturated fat); 25.4kJ (599 cal); 88.8g carbohydrate; 13.5g protein; 10.5g fibre

Lasagne bolognese

2 teaspoons olive oil
6 slices pancetta (90g), chopped
1 large onion (200g), chopped
1 medium carrot (120g),
    chopped finely
2 stalks celery (300g), trimmed,
    chopped finely
1kg (2 pounds) minced
    (ground) beef
150g (5 ounces) chicken livers,
    trimmed, chopped finely
2 cups (500ml) milk
60g (2 ounces) butter
2 cups (500ml) beef stock

1 cup (250ml) dry red wine
410g (13 ounces) canned
    tomato puree
2 tablespoons tomato paste
¼ cup finely chopped fresh
    flat-leaf parsley
6 sheets fresh lasagne (300g)
2 cups (160g) finely grated
    parmesan cheese
white sauce
125g (4 ounces) butter
¾ cup (110g) plain (all-purpose)
    flour
1.25 litres (5 cups) hot milk

1 Heat oil in large heavy-based pan; cook pancetta, stirring, until crisp.
Add onion, carrot and celery; cook, stirring, until vegetables soften. Add
mince and liver; cook, stirring, until beef just changes colour. Stir in milk
and butter; cook, stirring occasionally, until liquid reduces to about half.
Add stock, wine, puree and paste; simmer, uncovered, 1½ hours. Remove
from heat; stir in parsley.
2 Preheat oven to 200°C/400°F. Oil deep 25cm x 35cm (10-inch x
14-inch) baking dish.
3 Make white sauce.
4 Spread about ½ cup of the white sauce over base of dish. Layer
two pasta sheets, a quarter of the meat sauce, ¼ cup of the cheese
and about 1 cup of the remaining white sauce in dish. Repeat layering
process, starting with pasta sheets and ending with white sauce; you
will have four layers in total. Top lasagne with the remaining cheese.
5 Bake lasagne about 40 minutes or until top is browned lightly.
Stand 15 minutes before serving.
white sauce Melt butter in medium saucepan; add flour, stirring until
mixture forms a smooth paste. Stir in milk gradually; bring to the boil,
stirring, until sauce boils and thickens.

prep + cook time 4 hours (+ standing) **serves** 8
nutritional count per serving 44.3g total fat (26.3g saturated fat);
3269kJ (782 cal); 33.7g carbohydrate; 52.9g protein; 3.2g fibre

Beef and eggplant parmigiana lasagne

1 tablespoon olive oil
1 medium brown onion (150g), chopped finely
1 clove garlic, crushed
1kg (2 pounds) minced (ground) beef
½ cup (125ml) dry red wine
2 cups (500ml) beef stock
2¾ cups (680ml) bottled tomato pasta sauce
¼ cup (70g) tomato paste
¾ cup finely chopped fresh basil
2 medium eggplants (600g), peeled, sliced thinly
cooking-oil spray
3 fresh lasagne sheets (150g)
2 cups (200g) coarsely grated mozzarella cheese
1 cup (100g) packaged breadcrumbs
½ cup (40g) coarsely grated parmesan cheese

1 Preheat oven to 200°C/400°F.
2 Heat oil in large frying pan; cook onion and garlic, stirring, until onion softens. Add mince; cook, stirring, until browned. Add wine, stock, sauce and paste; bring to the boil. Reduce heat; simmer, covered, 30 minutes, stirring occasionally. Uncover; simmer about 30 minutes or until slightly thickened; stir in basil.
3 Meanwhile, place eggplant on oiled oven tray; spray with oil. Roast about 20 minutes or until tender.
4 Oil shallow 2.5 litre (10-cup) ovenproof dish. Cover base with lasagne sheets, cut to fit; top with about one-third of the warm beef mixture, half the eggplant and ⅓ cup mozzarella.
5 Repeat layering with remaining trimmed lasagne sheets, another third of the beef mixture, remaining eggplant and ⅓ cup mozzarella; finishing with lasagne sheet. Spread remaining one-third of the beef mixture over lasagne; top with breadcrumbs, parmesan and remaining mozzarella. Bake lasagne, covered, 40 minutes.
6 Preheat grill (broiler). Uncover lasagne; place under grill until browned lightly. Stand 5 minutes before serving.

prep + cook time 2 hours 50 minutes **serves** 8
nutritional count per serving 20.9g total fat (8.9g saturated fat); 2123kJ (508 cal); 33.6g carbohydrate; 41g protein; 5.2g fibre

Vegetarian lasagne

2 cups (500ml) bottled tomato pasta sauce
3 fresh lasagne sheets (150g)
¾ cup (110g) drained semi-dried tomatoes in oil,
    chopped coarsely
90g (3-ounce) piece fetta cheese, crumbled
½ cup (120g) firm ricotta cheese, crumbled
1½ cups (180g) coarsely grated cheddar cheese
1 cup (150g) drained marinated char-grilled eggplant,
    chopped coarsely
¾ cup (165g) drained char-grilled capsicum (bell pepper)
125g (4 ounces) baby rocket (arugula) leaves

1 Preheat oven to 200°C/400°F. Oil shallow 2.5 litre (10-cup)
ovenproof dish.
2 Spread ½ cup pasta sauce over base of dish; top with a lasagne
sheet and another ½ cup pasta sauce. Top with semi-dried tomato,
¼ cup of each cheese, then another lasagne sheet. Top with ½ cup
pasta sauce, eggplant, remaining fetta, remaining ricotta and another
¼ cup cheddar. Top with remaining lasagne sheet, remaining sauce
and capsicum; sprinkle with remaining cheddar.
3 Bake lasagne, covered, 30 minutes. Uncover; bake 15 minutes.
Stand 5 minutes before serving; serve with rocket.

prep + cook time 55 minutes **serves** 4
nutritional count per serving 38.4g total fat (17.2g saturated fat);
2876kJ (688 cal); 49.6g carbohydrate; 31.4g protein; 9.9g fibre

Pork and veal lasagne

1 tablespoon olive oil
1 medium brown onion (150g),
  chopped coarsely
3 stalks celery (450g), trimmed,
  chopped coarsely
4 cloves garlic, crushed
2 teaspoons ground cinnamon
750g (1½ pounds) minced
  (ground) pork and veal
1 tablespoon plain (all-purpose) flour
2 tablespoons red wine vinegar
2 teaspoons brown sugar
2¾ cups (680ml) bottled tomato
  pasta sauce

410g (13 ounces) canned
  diced tomatoes
¼ cup finely chopped fresh sage
45g (1½ ounces) butter
2 tablespoons plain (all-purpose)
  flour, extra
2½ cups (625ml) hot milk
1½ cups (120g) finely grated
  parmesan cheese
250g (8 ounces) fresh lasagne
  sheets
2½ cups (250g) coarsely grated
  mozzarella cheese
12 fresh sage leaves

1 Heat oil in large saucepan; cook onion and celery, stirring, until soft.
Add garlic and cinnamon; cook, stirring, until fragrant.
2 Add mince; cook, stirring, until meat changes colour. Add flour; cook,
stirring, 1 minute. Stir in vinegar, sugar, pasta sauce and undrained
tomatoes; bring to the boil. Reduce heat; simmer, stirring occasionally,
about 15 minutes or until sauce thickens. Stir in chopped sage.
3 Preheat oven to 180°C/350°F.
4 Meanwhile, melt butter in medium saucepan. Add extra flour; cook,
stirring, until mixture thickens and bubbles. Gradually stir in milk; stir until
mixture boils and thickens. Remove sauce from heat; stir in one-third of
the parmesan.
5 Spread one-quarter of the meat sauce into shallow 20cm x 30cm
(8-inch x 12-inch) ovenproof dish. Cover with one-third of the trimmed
lasagne sheets, then one-third of the remaining meat sauce, half the
cheese sauce and half the mozzarella. Make two more layers with the
remaining lasagne and meat sauce; top with remaining cheese sauce.
Sprinkle with combined remaining cheeses, then sage leaves.
6 Bake lasagne, uncovered, about 50 minutes or until browned lightly.
Stand 15 minutes before serving.

prep + cook time 1 hour 30 minutes (+ standing) **serves** 6
nutritional count per serving 39.3g total fat (20.5g saturated fat);
3428kJ (820 cal); 55.2g carbohydrate; 58.3g protein; 6.3g fibre

Spinach and ricotta cannelloni

1kg (2 pounds) spinach, trimmed, chopped coarsely
500g (1 pound) ricotta cheese
2 eggs
¼ cup finely chopped fresh mint
2 teaspoons finely chopped fresh thyme
2 teaspoons finely chopped fresh rosemary
1½ cups (120g) coarsely grated parmesan cheese
250g (8 ounces) cannelloni tubes
creamy tomato sauce
1 tablespoon olive oil
1 medium brown onion (150g), chopped finely
4 cloves garlic, crushed
2 x 800g (28 ounces) canned diced tomatoes
½ cup (125ml) pouring cream
1 teaspoon white sugar

1 Make creamy tomato sauce.
2 Meanwhile, preheat oven to 180°C/350°F.
3 Cook washed, drained spinach in heated large saucepan, stirring, until wilted. Drain; when cool enough to handle, squeeze out excess moisture.
4 Combine spinach in large bowl with ricotta, eggs, herbs and ½ cup of the parmesan. Using a large piping bag, fill tubes with spinach mixture.
5 Spread one-third of the sauce into shallow 25cm x 35cm (10-inch x 14-inch) ovenproof dish; top with cannelloni, in single layer, then top with remaining sauce. Bake, covered, 20 minutes. Uncover, sprinkle with remaining parmesan; bake further 15 minutes or until pasta is tender and cheese is browned lightly.
creamy tomato sauce Heat oil in large saucepan; cook onion, stirring, until softened. Add garlic; cook, stirring, until fragrant. Add undrained tomatoes; bring to the boil. Reduce heat; simmer, uncovered, stirring occasionally, about 20 minutes or until sauce thickens slightly. Cool 10 minutes. Blend or process sauce with cream and sugar until smooth.

prep + cook time 1 hour **serves** 6
nutritional count per serving 31g total fat (17.1g saturated fat); 2412kJ (577 cal); 41.8g carbohydrate; 28.7g protein; 8.3g fibre

Spaghetti bolognese

2 teaspoons olive oil
6 slices pancetta (90g), chopped finely
1 large white onion (200g), chopped finely
1 medium carrot (120g), chopped finely
2 stalks celery (300g) trimmed, chopped finely
625g (1¼ pounds) minced (ground) beef
155g (5 ounces) chicken livers, trimmed, chopped finely
1 cup (250ml) milk
60g (2 ounces) butter
1½ cups (375ml) beef stock
1 cup (250ml) dry red wine
410g (13 ounces) canned tomato puree
2 tablespoons tomato paste
¼ cup finely chopped fresh flat-leaf parsley
750g (1½ pounds) fresh spaghetti
½ cup (40g) shaved parmesan cheese

1 Heat oil in large heavy-based frying pan; cook pancetta, stirring, until crisp. Add onion, carrot and celery; cook, stirring, until vegetables soften.
2 Add beef and liver to pan; cook, stirring, until beef changes colour. Stir in milk and butter; cook, stirring occasionally, until liquid reduces to about half.
3 Add stock, wine, puree and paste to pan; simmer, covered, 1 hour. Uncover; simmer 1 hour. Remove from heat; stir in parsley.
4 Meanwhile, cook pasta in large saucepan of boiling water until tender; drain.
5 Serve pasta topped with sauce and cheese.

prep + cook time 2 hours 35 minutes **serves** 6
nutritional count per serving 26.6g total fat (13g saturated fat); 2504kJ (599 cal); 41g carbohydrate; 39.2g protein; 5.5g fibre
tip You can substitute 500g (1 pound) dried spaghetti for the fresh spaghetti, if you prefer.

Broccoli and garlic breadcrumb spaghetti

12 slices stale white bread
500g (1 pound) spaghetti
280g (9 ounces) broccoli, cut into florets
⅓ cup (80ml) olive oil
45g (1½ ounces) butter
2 cloves garlic, crushed
¼ cup (20g) shaved parmesan cheese

1 Remove and discard crusts from bread; process bread until fine.
2 Cook pasta in large saucepan of boiling water until tender; drain.
3 Meanwhile, boil, steam or microwave broccoli until tender; drain.
4 Heat oil and butter in large frying pan; cook breadcrumbs and garlic until browned lightly and crisp.
5 Combine pasta, broccoli and breadcrumb mixture in large bowl; serve topped with cheese.

prep + cook time 25 minutes **serves** 4
nutritional count per serving 34.2g total fat (11g saturated fat); 4004kJ (958 cal); 129g carbohydrate; 27.7g protein; 10.2g fibre

Spaghetti with clams

1kg (2 pounds) clams
¼ cup (60ml) dry white wine
500g (1 pound) spaghetti
½ cup (125ml) extra virgin olive oil
2 cloves garlic, crushed
2 fresh medium red chillies, chopped
½ cup coarsely chopped fresh flat-leaf parsley

1 Rinse clams. Place in bowl of cold water; stand 1 hour. Drain.
2 Bring wine to the boil in large saucepan. Add clams to pan; simmer, covered, until shells open. Remove clams from pan; cover to keep warm. Strain cooking liquid through a fine sieve into a jug; reserve ½ cup of the liquid.
3 Meanwhile, cook spaghetti in large saucepan of boiling water until tender; drain. Return spaghetti to pan.
4 Heat oil in large frying pan; cook garlic and chilli, stirring, until fragrant. Add clams to spaghetti with oil mixture, parsley and enough of the reserved cooking liquid to moisten; toss gently to combine.

prep + cook time 30 minutes (+ standing) **serves** 4
nutritional count per serving 14.4g total fat (2.1g saturated fat); 1455kJ (348 cal); 41.2g carbohydrate; 11g protein; 2.3g fibre

Spaghetti with pesto

2 cloves garlic, chopped coarsely
⅓ cup (50g) roasted pine nuts
½ cup (40g) finely grated parmesan cheese
2 cups firmly packed fresh basil leaves
½ cup (125ml) olive oil
500g (1 pound) spaghetti
½ cup (40g) shaved parmesan cheese

1 Blend or process garlic, nuts, grated cheese and basil until almost smooth. Gradually add oil in a thin, steady stream, processing until thick.
2 Cook pasta in large saucepan of boiling water until just tender; drain, reserving ¼ cup of the cooking liquid.
3 Combine pasta, pesto and reserved cooking liquid in large bowl. Serve with shaved cheese.

prep + cook time 25 minutes **serves** 4
nutritional count per serving 45.2g total fat (8.9g saturated fat); 3578kJ (859 cal); 86.2g carbohydrate; 23.6g protein; 5.6g fibre

Spaghetti and meatballs

500g (1 pound) minced (ground) pork and veal
½ cup (35g) stale breadcrumbs
1 egg
¼ cup (20g) finely grated parmesan cheese
1 tablespoon olive oil
1 medium brown onion (150g), chopped coarsely
2 cloves garlic, quartered
1 fresh small red thai chilli
6 anchovy fillets
1 cup (150g) drained sun-dried tomatoes
¼ cup (70g) tomato paste
1 cup (250ml) chicken stock
12 pimiento-stuffed olives, sliced thinly
375g (12 ounces) spaghetti
⅓ cup coarsely chopped fresh flat-leaf parsley

1 Combine mince, breadcrumbs, egg and cheese in medium bowl; roll level tablespoons of mixture into balls.
2 Heat oil in medium frying pan; cook meatballs, uncovered, until browned.
3 Blend or process onion, garlic, chilli, anchovy, tomatoes and paste until smooth.
4 Combine onion mixture and stock in medium saucepan; bring to the boil. Add meatballs and olives; simmer, uncovered, 15 minutes.
5 Meanwhile, cook pasta in large saucepan of boiling water until tender; drain.
6 Serve spaghetti topped with meatballs and sauce; sprinkle with parsley.

prep + cook time 35 minutes **serves** 4
nutritional count per serving 20.6g total fat (6.3g saturated fat); 2964kJ (709 cal); 78.8g carbohydrate; 47.5g protein; 7.9g fibre

Fusilli amatriciana

500g (1 pound) fusilli pasta
¼ cup (60ml) olive oil
200g (6½ ounces) pancetta, chopped finely
½ teaspoon dried chilli flakes
3 cups (750ml) bottled tomato pasta sauce
¼ cup loosely packed fresh basil leaves
⅓ cup (25g) finely grated parmesan cheese
⅓ cup (25g) finely grated pecorino cheese

1 Cook pasta in large saucepan of boiling water until tender; drain.
2 Heat half the oil in large saucepan; cook pancetta, stirring, until browned. Add chilli, sauce and basil; bring to the boil, then reduce heat. Stir in remaining oil.
3 Just before serving, combine pasta with sauce and cheeses.

prep + cook time 35 minutes **serves** 4
nutritional count per serving 26.3g total fat (7.3g saturated fat); 3294kJ (788 cal); 100.3g carbohydrate; 32.9g protein; 7.2g fibre

Penne with char-grilled capsicum and pine nuts

2 large red capsicums (bell peppers) (700g)
375g (12 ounces) penne pasta
2 tablespoons olive oil
2 cloves garlic, crushed
½ cup (80g) roasted pine nuts
2 fresh small red thai chillies, chopped finely
¼ cup (60ml) lemon juice
125g (4 ounces) baby rocket (arugula) leaves
125g (4 ounces) fetta cheese, crumbled

1 Quarter capsicums; discard seeds and membranes. Roast under grill or in very hot oven, skin-side up, until skin blisters and blackens. Cover capsicum pieces in plastic or paper for 5 minutes, peel away skin then slice thinly.
2 Cook pasta in large saucepan of boiling water until just tender; drain.
3 Meanwhile, heat oil in large frying pan; cook garlic, nuts and chilli, stirring, about 2 minutes or until fragrant. Add capsicum and juice; stir until hot.
4 Place pasta and capsicum mixture in large bowl with rocket and cheese; toss gently to combine.

prep + cook time 35 minutes **serves** 4
nutritional count per serving 30.5g total fat (6.2g saturated fat); 2755kJ (659 cal); 74.4g carbohydrate; 21g protein; 8.2g fibre

Chicken, mushroom and asparagus creamy pasta bake

375g (12 ounces) rigatoni pasta
60g (2 ounces) butter
625g (1¼ pounds) chicken breast fillets,
    cut into 1cm (½-inch) pieces
125g (4 ounces) button mushrooms, sliced thinly
2 tablespoons plain (all-purpose) flour
2 cups (500ml) milk
½ cup (40g) coarsely grated romano cheese
1¼ cups (150g) coarsely grated cheddar
185g (6 ounces) asparagus, trimmed, chopped coarsely
¼ cup coarsely chopped fresh flat-leaf parsley

1 Preheat oven to 200°C/400°F.
2 Cook pasta in large saucepan of boiling water until just tender; drain.
3 Meanwhile, heat one-third of the butter in large frying pan; cook chicken, in batches, until browned and cooked through. Remove from pan.
4 Heat remaining butter in same pan; cook mushrooms, stirring, until tender. Add flour; cook, stirring, 1 minute. Gradually stir in milk. Stir over medium heat until mixture boils and thickens. Stir in chicken, ¼ cup of the romano, ¾ cup of the cheddar and asparagus.
5 Combine chicken mixture and pasta in 2.5 litre (10-cup) ovenproof dish; sprinkle with remaining cheeses. Bake about 15 minutes or until top browns lightly. Serve pasta bake sprinkled with parsley.

prep + cook time 50 minutes **serves** 4
nutritional count per serving 37.3g total fat (22.3g saturated fat); 3775kJ (903 cal); 75.2g carbohydrate; 64g protein; 4.8g fibre

Penne puttanesca

500g (1 pound) penne pasta
4 whole anchovy fillets, drained
¼ cup (60ml) olive oil
1 fresh long red chilli, sliced thinly
3 cups (750ml) bottled tomato pasta sauce
1 cup (120g) seeded black olives
2 tablespoons drained baby capers, rinsed,
  chopped coarsely

1 Cook pasta in large saucepan of boiling water until tender; drain.
2 Finely chop anchovy fillets. Using side of heavy knife, press down firmly on anchovy to crush.
3 Heat 1 tablespoon of the oil in large saucepan; cook anchovy and chilli, stirring, 2 minutes. Add sauce; bring to the boil. Stir in olives, capers and remaining oil. Reduce heat; simmer, uncovered, 5 minutes or until heated through.
4 Serve pasta topped with sauce.

prep + cook time 30 minutes **serves** 4
nutritional count per serving 17.4g total fat (2.5g saturated fat); 2876kJ (688 cal); 107.4g carbohydrate; 20.4g protein; 7.7g fibre

Farfalle with chicken, spinach and tomato

375g (12 ounces) farfalle pasta
1 tablespoon olive oil
1 medium brown onion (150g), chopped finely
1 clove garlic, crushed
625g (1¼ pounds) chicken tenderloins, chopped coarsely
150g (5 ounces) baby spinach leaves
1 cup (200g) ricotta cheese
1 egg
2 teaspoons finely grated lemon rind
2 tablespoons lemon juice
200g (6½ ounces) grape tomatoes, halved
¼ cup (20g) finely grated parmesan cheese

1 Cook pasta in large saucepan of boiling water until just tender; drain.
2 Meanwhile, heat oil in large deep frying pan; cook onion and garlic, stirring, until onion softens. Add chicken; cook, stirring, over medium heat, about 5 minutes or until chicken is cooked through.
3 Place pasta and chicken mixture in large serving bowl with spinach, combined ricotta and egg, rind, juice and tomato; toss gently to combine.
4 Serve pasta sprinkled with parmesan.

prep + cook time 25 minutes **serves** 4
nutritional count per serving 20.7g total fat (7.7g saturated fat);
2851kJ (682 cal); 67.7g carbohydrate; 52.2g protein; 5.6g fibre

Broad bean and ricotta orecchiette

375g (12 ounces) orecchiette pasta
1 tablespoon olive oil
2 cups (300g) fresh shelled broad beans
1 clove garlic, crushed
½ cup (125ml) pouring cream
1 teaspoon finely grated lemon rind
2 tablespoons lemon juice
200g (6½ ounces) ricotta cheese, crumbled
½ cup coarsely chopped fresh mint

1 Cook pasta in large saucepan of boiling water until tender; drain.
2 Meanwhile, heat oil in large frying pan; cook beans and garlic until beans are just tender. Add cream, rind and juice; simmer, uncovered, until sauce thickens slightly.
3 Place pasta and sauce in large bowl with remaining ingredients; toss gently to combine.

prep + cook time 30 minutes **serves** 4
nutritional count per serving 25.2g total fat (13.4g saturated fat); 2500kJ (598 cal); 67.4g carbohydrate; 21.3g protein; 7.9g fibre

Ravioli arrabbiata

500g (1 pound) ravioli pasta
¼ cup (60ml) olive oil
2 fresh small red thai chillies, chopped finely
3 cups (750ml) bottled tomato pasta sauce
½ cup coarsely chopped fresh flat-leaf parsley

1 Cook pasta in large saucepan of boiling water until tender; drain.
2 Heat half the oil in large saucepan; cook chilli, stirring, 2 minutes. Add sauce; bring to the boil. Stir in remaining oil and parsley.
3 Serve pasta topped with sauce.

prep + cook time 25 minutes **serves** 4
nutritional count per serving 21.4g total fat (4.6g saturated fat); 1672kJ (400 cal); 37g carbohydrate; 12.3g protein; 5.7g fibre

Pumpkin ravioli and roasted tomato salad

500g (1 pound) cherry tomatoes, halved
2 medium red onions (340g), halved, sliced thinly
1 teaspoon caster (superfine) sugar
¼ cup (60ml) olive oil
1kg (2 pounds) pumpkin ravioli pasta
125g (4 ounces) baby rocket (arugula) leaves
155g (5 ounces) small black olives, seeded
2 tablespoons drained baby capers, rinsed
2 tablespoons red wine vinegar

1 Preheat oven to 220°C/425°F. Line oven tray with baking paper.
2 Place tomato and onion, in single layer, on tray; sprinkle with sugar, drizzle with 1 tablespoon of the oil. Roast about 20 minutes.
3 Meanwhile, cook pasta in large saucepan of boiling water until tender; drain.
4 Place pasta in large bowl with tomato, onion, rocket, olives and capers; toss gently to combine. Drizzle with combined vinegar and remaining oil.

prep + cook time 30 minutes **serves** 6
nutritional count per serving 18g total fat (4.7g saturated fat); 1542kJ (369 cal); 35g carbohydrate; 14.3g protein; 5.2g fibre

Warm agnolotti and salmon salad

1 cup (120g) frozen peas
185g (6 ounces) asparagus, trimmed, chopped coarsely
500g (1-pound) piece salmon fillet
625g (1¼ pounds) spinach and ricotta agnolotti pasta
½ cup fresh flat-leaf parsley leaves
1 tablespoon water
¼ cup (60ml) olive oil
1 teaspoon finely grated lemon rind
¼ cup (60ml) lemon juice

1 Boil, steam or microwave peas and asparagus, separately, until just tender; drain. Rinse under cold water; drain.
2 Cook fish on heated oiled grill plate (or grill or grill pan) until browned both sides and cooked as desired. Place fish in large bowl; using fork, flake into chunks.
3 Meanwhile, cook pasta in large saucepan of boiling water until just tender; drain. Add pasta to fish.
4 Combine parsley, the water, oil, rind and juice in small jug; pour over fish and pasta. Add peas and asparagus; toss gently to combine.

prep + cook time 35 minutes **serves** 4
nutritional count per serving 33.7g total fat (10.6g saturated fat); 2428kJ (581 cal); 26.9g carbohydrate; 39.8g protein; 5.5g fibre

Gnocchi with roasted kumara, spinach and pine nuts

1.5kg (3 pounds) potatoes, unpeeled
¼ cup (60ml) milk
1 clove garlic, crushed
3 egg yolks
½ cup (40g) finely grated parmesan cheese
1½ cups (225g) plain (all-purpose) flour
2 medium kumara (orange sweet potato) (800g), cut into 1cm (½-inch) pieces

2 tablespoons olive oil
200g (6½ ounces) unsalted butter, chopped
3 medium tomatoes (450g), chopped finely
¾ cup loosely packed fresh sage leaves
60g (2 ounces) baby spinach leaves
½ cup (40g) shaved parmesan cheese
⅓ cup (50g) roasted pine nuts

1 Boil or steam whole potatoes until tender; drain. Peel when cool enough to handle. Mash, using ricer or food mill (mouli) into large bowl; stir in milk, garlic, egg yolks, grated cheese and flour to make a firm dough.
2 Divide dough into four equal portions; roll each portion on floured surface into 2cm (¾-inch) thick sausage-shape. Cut each sausage-shape into 2cm (¾-inch) pieces; roll each piece along the tines of a fork, pressing lightly with index finger to form classic gnocchi shape (grooved on one side, dimpled on the other). Place gnocchi, in single layer, on floured tray. Cover; refrigerate 1 hour.
3 Preheat oven to 200°C/400°F. Combine kumara and half the oil in shallow medium baking dish; roast about 30 minutes or until tender.
4 Cook gnocchi in large saucepan of boiling salted water about 3 minutes or until gnocchi float to the surface. Remove from pan with slotted spoon; drain.
5 Melt butter in medium frying pan with remaining oil; cook tomato and sage, stirring, 2 minutes or until tomato softens slightly and butter is browned lightly.
6 Combine gnocchi, kumara, tomato mixture and remaining ingredients in large bowl. Serve gnocchi topped with extra shaved parmesan, if you like.

prep + cook time 1 hour 30 minutes (+ refrigeration) **serves** 6
nutritional count per serving 45.5g total fat (21.8g saturated fat); 3302kJ (790 cal); 74.5g carbohydrate; 18g protein; 8.5g fibre

Gnocchi with three cheeses

1kg (2 pounds) russet burbank potatoes, unpeeled
2 eggs, beaten lightly
30g butter, melted
¼ cup (20g) finely grated parmesan cheese
2 cups (300g) plain (all-purpose) flour, approximately
three-cheese sauce
60g butter
⅓ cup (50g) plain (all-purpose) flour
2 cups (500ml) milk
1¼ cups (310ml) pouring cream
60g (2 ounces) coarsely grated provolone cheese
70g (2½ ounces) coarsely grated fontina cheese
40g (1½ ounces) gorgonzola cheese, crumbled

1 Boil or steam whole potatoes until tender; drain. Peel when cool
enough to handle. Mash, using ricer or food mill (mouli) into large bowl;
stir in egg, butter, cheese and enough of the flour to make a firm dough.
2 Divide dough into eight equal portions; roll each portion on floured
surface into 2cm (¾-inch) thick sausage-shape. Cut each sausage-shape
into 2cm (¾-inch) pieces; roll pieces into balls. Roll each ball along the
tines of a fork, pressing lightly on top of ball with index finger to form
classic gnocchi shape (grooved on one side, dimpled on the other).
Place gnocchi, in single layer, on floured tray. Cover; refrigerate 1 hour.
3 Meanwhile, make three-cheese sauce.
4 Cook gnocchi in large saucepan of boiling salted water about 3 minutes
or until gnocchi float to the surface. Remove from pan with slotted spoon;
drain. Serve gnocchi immediately with sauce; sprinkle with chopped fresh
flat-leaf parsley, if you like.
three-cheese sauce Melt butter in medium saucepan. Add flour; cook,
stirring, until mixture thickens and bubbles. Gradually add milk and cream;
stir until mixture boils and thickens. Remove from heat; stir in cheeses.

prep + cook time 1 hour 15 minutes (+ refrigeration) **serves** 8
nutritional count per serving 37.5g total fat (23.8g saturated fat);
2638kJ (631 cal); 52.2g carbohydrate; 19.5g protein; 4.2g fibre
tip You can use a 300ml carton of cream without affecting the recipe.

First Courses

Beef carpaccio

400g (13-ounce) piece beef eye fillet
2 tablespoons olive oil
2 teaspoons finely grated lemon rind
2 tablespoons lemon juice
1 clove garlic, crushed
⅓ cup finely chopped fresh flat-leaf parsley
2 tablespoons finely chopped fresh oregano
⅓ cup finely chopped baby rocket (arugula) leaves
⅓ cup (25g) shaved parmesan cheese.

1 Tightly wrap beef fillet in plastic wrap; freeze 1 hour or until firm.
2 Unwrap beef; slice as thinly as possible. Arrange slices on platter.
3 Combine oil, rind, juice, garlic, herbs and rocket in small bowl.
4 Serve beef sprinkled with herb mixture and cheese.

prep time 30 minutes (+ freezing) **serves** 8
nutritional count per serving 7.8g total fat (2.3g saturated fat);
506kJ (121 cal); 0.3g carbohydrate; 12.3g protein; 0.3g fibre

Tuna carpaccio

400g (13-ounce) piece sashimi tuna
¼ cup (60ml) lime juice
2 tablespoons olive oil
1 fresh long red chilli, chopped finely
¼ cup finely shredded fresh basil
2 tablespoons coarsely chopped roasted pistachios

1 Tightly wrap tuna in plastic wrap; freeze 1 hour.
2 Unwrap tuna; slice as thinly as possible. Arrange slices on platter; drizzle tuna with juice. Cover; refrigerate 1 hour.
3 Combine oil, chilli, basil and pistachios in medium bowl.
4 Drain juice from tuna; serve tuna topped with basil mixture.

prep time 30 minutes (+ freezing & refrigeration) **serves** 8
nutritional count per serving 8.3g total fat (1.9g saturated fat); 535kJ (128 cal); 0.4g carbohydrate; 13g protein; 0.2g fibre

Garlic prawns

1kg (1 pound) uncooked medium king prawns (shrimp)
4 cloves garlic, crushed
2 fresh small red thai chillies, chopped finely
2 tablespoons olive oil
1 medium red capsicum (bell pepper) (200g), sliced thinly
1 medium green capsicum (bell pepper) (200g), sliced thinly
½ cup (125ml) chicken stock
1¼ cups (310ml) pouring cream
1 tablespoon lemon juice
1 tablespoon finely chopped fresh flat-leaf parsley

1 Shell and devein prawns, leaving tails intact. Combine prawns,
garlic and chilli in medium bowl.
2 Heat half the oil in large frying pan; cook prawns, stirring, until
changed in colour. Remove from pan.
3 Heat remaining oil in same pan; cook capsicums, stirring, until tender.
4 Return prawns to pan with stock, cream and juice; bring to the boil.
Reduce heat; simmer, uncovered, about 5 minutes or until sauce thickens
slightly. Remove from heat; stir in parsley.

prep + cook time 30 minutes **serves** 4
nutritional count per serving 42.6g total fat (22.9g saturated fat);
2169kJ (519 cal); 5.4g carbohydrate; 28.9g protein; 1.4g fibre
tip You can use a 300ml carton of cream without affecting the recipe.

Pan-seared scallops with anchovy butter

2 teaspoons olive oil
12 scallops (300g), roe removed
30g (1 ounce) butter
3 drained anchovy fillets
2 cloves garlic, crushed
2 teaspoons lemon juice
1 tablespoon finely chopped fresh chives

1 Heat oil in large frying pan; cook scallops, both sides, until browned lightly. Remove from pan; cover to keep warm.
2 Cook butter, anchovies and garlic in same pan; stirring, until garlic is browned lightly. Return scallops to pan with juice; cook until scallops are heated through.
3 Serve scallops drizzled with anchovy butter and sprinkled with chives.

prep + cook time 15 minutes **serves** 4
nutritional count per serving 9.1g total fat (4.8g saturated fat); 514kJ (123 cal); 0.8g carbohydrate; 9.6g protein; 0.3g fibre

Char-grilled cuttlefish, rocket and parmesan salad

1kg (1 pound) cuttlefish hoods
2 tablespoons olive oil
1 tablespoon finely grated lemon rind
⅓ cup (80ml) lemon juice
1 clove garlic, crushed
150g (5 ounces) rocket (arugula)
150g (5 ounces) semi-dried tomatoes, drained, chopped coarsely
1 small red onion (100g), sliced thinly
1 tablespoon drained baby capers, rinsed
75g (2½ ounces) parmesan cheese, shaved
2 tablespoons balsamic vinegar
⅓ cup (80ml) olive oil, extra

1 Halve cuttlefish lengthways, score insides in crosshatch pattern then cut into 5cm (2-inch) strips. Combine cuttlefish with oil, rind, juice and garlic in medium bowl. Cover; refrigerate 10 minutes.
2 Meanwhile, combine rocket, tomato, onion, capers and cheese in large serving bowl.
3 Drain cuttlefish; discard marinade. Cook cuttlefish, in batches, on heated oiled grill plate (or grill or grill pan) until browned and cooked through.
4 Add cuttlefish to salad with combined vinegar and extra oil; toss gently to combine.

prep + cook time 30 minutes **serves** 4
nutritional count per serving 36.9g total fat (7.9g saturated fat); 2203kJ (527 cal); 16.5g carbohydrate; 30g protein; 6.7g fibre

Barbecued seafood

16 uncooked medium king prawns (shrimp) (720g)
1 teaspoon finely grated lemon rind
½ teaspoon dried chilli flakes
1 clove garlic, crushed
1 tablespoon finely chopped fresh oregano
2 tablespoons olive oil
8 slices prosciutto (120g)
8 butterflied sardines (240g)
280g (9 ounces) baby octopus, quartered
200g (6½ ounces) squid hoods, sliced into rings
2 tablespoons balsamic vinegar
¼ cup coarsely chopped fresh flat-leaf parsley
500g (1 pound) small black mussels
¼ cup (60ml) lemon juice
1 medium tomato (150g), seeded, chopped finely

1 Remove and discard prawn heads. Cut prawns lengthways, three-quarters of the way through, (and down to 1cm/½ inch before the tail) leaving shells intact; press down on prawns on board to flatten.
2 Combine prawns, rind, chilli, garlic, oregano and half the oil in medium bowl. Cover; refrigerate 1 hour.
3 Wrap a prosciutto slice firmly around each sardine.
4 Cook octopus and squid on heated oiled grill plate (or grill or grill pan). Combine octopus and squid in medium heatproof bowl with remaining oil, vinegar and 2 tablespoons of the parsley. Cover to keep warm.
5 Cook prawns and sardines on heated oiled grill plate (or grill or grill pan).
6 Meanwhile, cook mussels, covered, on heated oiled flat plate about 5 minutes or until mussels open (discard any that do not). Place mussels in medium heatproof bowl; drizzle with juice, sprinkle with tomato and remaining parsley. Serve seafood with lemon wedges, if you like.

prep + cook time 1 hour (+ refrigeration) **serves** 8
nutritional count per serving 8.7g total fat (1.7g saturated fat);
836kJ (200 cal); 1.3g carbohydrate; 28.5g protein; 0.4g fibre

Sardines with caper and parsley gremolata

8 sardines (360g), cleaned
⅓ cup (50g) self-raising flour
½ teaspoon sweet paprika
olive oil, for shallow-frying
caper and parsley gremolata
2 tablespoons drained baby capers, rinsed, chopped finely
1 clove garlic, crushed
¼ cup finely chopped fresh flat-leaf parsley
2 teaspoons finely grated lemon rind
2 teaspoons lemon juice

1 Make caper and parsley gremolata.
2 To butterfly sardines, cut through the underside of the fish to the tail. Break backbone at tail; peel away backbone. Trim sardines.
3 Coat fish in combined flour and paprika; shake away excess. Heat oil in large frying pan; shallow-fry fish, in batches, until cooked through. Remove from pan; drain on absorbent paper.
4 Sprinkle fish with topping. Serve with lemon wedges, if you like.
caper and parsley gremolata Combine ingredients in small bowl.

prep + cook time 45 minutes **serves** 8
nutritional count per serving 4.6g total fat (0.9g saturated fat); 376kJ (90 cal); 4.8g carbohydrate; 7.1g protein; 0.5g fibre

White wine risotto cakes with smoked chicken

2¾ cups (680ml) chicken stock
15g (½ ounce) butter
1 tablespoon olive oil
1 small brown onion (80g), chopped finely
1 clove garlic, crushed
⅔ cup (130g) arborio rice
¼ cup (60ml) dry white wine
¼ cup (20g) coarsely grated parmesan cheese

2 tablespoons finely shredded fresh basil
1 tablespoon dijon mustard
1 tablespoon sour cream
2 tablespoons vegetable oil
32 baby rocket (arugula) leaves
185g (6 ounces) smoked chicken breast, shredded coarsely

1 Place stock in medium saucepan; bring to the boil. Reduce heat; simmer, covered.

2 Meanwhile, heat butter and half the olive oil in medium saucepan; cook onion and garlic, stirring, until onion just softens. Add rice; stir rice to coat in onion mixture. Add wine; cook, stirring, until wine is almost evaporated. Stir in ½ cup simmering stock; cook, stirring, over low heat until liquid is absorbed. Continue adding stock, in ½-cup batches, stirring until liquid is absorbed after each addition. Total cooking time should be about 30 minutes or until rice is tender. Gently stir in cheese and basil; cool 20 minutes.

3 Divide risotto into four portions; using hands, shape portions into 1cm (½-inch) deep patty-shaped cakes. Cover; refrigerate 30 minutes.

4 Meanwhile, combine mustard and sour cream in small bowl.

5 Heat vegetable oil in large frying pan; cook risotto cakes, uncovered, until browned both sides and heated through.

6 Place each risotto cake on serving plate; top each with 8 rocket leaves, a quarter of the chicken then 2 teaspoons of the mustard mixture; drizzle with remaining olive oil.

prep + cook time 1 hour 10 minutes (+ cooling & refrigeration)
serves 4
nutritional count per serving 23.4g total fat (6.7g saturated fat); 1676kJ (401 cal); 28.4g carbohydrate; 17.4g protein; 1g fibre

Caramelised fennel tarts

45g (1½ ounces) butter
4 baby fennel bulbs (520g), trimmed, halved lengthways
1 teaspoon finely grated orange rind
½ cup (125ml) orange juice
1 sheet puff pastry
2 teaspoons finely chopped fresh thyme

1 Preheat oven to 220°C/425°F. Grease two oven trays; line with baking paper.
2 Melt butter in large frying pan; cook fennel until browned lightly. Add rind and juice; bring to the boil. Reduce heat; simmer, uncovered, about 5 minutes or until fennel is caramelised and tender.
3 Cut pastry sheet into four squares; place on oven trays. Remove fennel from pan, leaving behind the pan juices; divide among pastry squares. Bake tarts about 20 minutes or until pastry is browned.
4 Meanwhile, return pan juices to the boil. Reduce heat; simmer, uncovered, until sauce thickens slightly.
5 Serve tarts drizzled with sauce and sprinkled with thyme.

prep + cook time 45 minutes **serves** 4
nutritional count per serving 19.8g total fat (11.9 saturated fat); 1145kJ (274 cal); 19.9g carbohydrate; 3.3g protein; 2.7g fibre

Tuscan white bean salad

2 x 400g (13 ounces) canned white beans, rinsed, drained
1 medium red onion (170g), chopped finely
⅔ cup (100g) drained semi-dried tomatoes in oil
150g (5 ounces) mozzarella cheese, cut into 1cm (½-inch) pieces
½ cup (75g) seeded kalamata olives
150g (5 ounces) rocket (arugula)
oregano balsamic vinaigrette
1 clove garlic, crushed
1 tablespoon finely chopped fresh oregano
¼ cup (60ml) balsamic vinegar
¼ cup (60ml) extra virgin olive oil

1 Make oregano balsamic vinaigrette.
2 Place beans, onion, tomato, cheese and olives in medium bowl with vinaigrette; toss gently to combine.
3 Serve bean salad with rocket.
oregano balsamic vinaigrette Place ingredients in screw-top jar; shake well.

prep + cook time 20 minutes **serves** 4
nutritional count per serving 23.8g total fat (7.5g saturated fat); 1563kJ (374 cal); 19.3g carbohydrate; 17.3g protein; 7.8g fibre

Roasted capsicum and ricotta salad

2 medium orange capsicums (bell pepper) (400g)
2 medium red capsicums (bell pepper) (400g)
2 medium yellow capsicums (bell pepper) (400g)
2 medium green capsicums (bell pepper) (400g)
75g (2½ ounces) baby rocket (arugula) leaves
1 small red onion (100g), sliced thinly
1 cup (240g) ricotta cheese, crumbled
oregano vinaigrette
⅓ cup (80ml) olive oil
2 tablespoons red wine vinegar
1 clove garlic, crushed
1 tablespoon finely chopped fresh oregano

1 Preheat oven to 200°C/400°F.
2 Quarter capsicums; discard seeds and membranes. Place capsicum, skin-side up, on oven tray. Roast, uncovered, about 20 minutes or until skin blisters and blackens. Cover capsicum pieces with plastic or paper for 5 minutes; peel away skin, then slice capsicum thickly.
3 Make oregano vinaigrette.
4 Combine capsicum with rocket and onion in large bowl; sprinkle with cheese, drizzle with vinaigrette.
oregano vinaigrette Place ingredients in screw-top jar; shake well.

prep + cook time 30 minutes **serves** 4
nutritional count per serving 25.6g total fat (6.9g saturated fat); 1396kJ (334 cal); 12.4g carbohydrate; 12.3g protein; 3.9g fibre

Witlof, pear and blue cheese salad

2 red witlof (belgian endive) (250g), trimmed, leaves separated
2 yellow witlof (belgian endive) (250g), trimmed, leaves separated
1 medium pear (230g), sliced thinly
¾ cup (90g) roasted pecans, coarsely chopped
blue cheese dressing
⅓ cup (80ml) buttermilk
100g (3 ounces) blue cheese, crumbled
1 tablespoon lemon juice

1 Make blue cheese dressing.
2 Combine salad ingredients in large bowl.
3 Serve salad drizzled with blue cheese dressing.
blue cheese dressing Whisk ingredients in small jug until smooth.

prep time 20 minutes **serves** 4
nutritional count per serving 24.9g total fat (6.5g saturated fat);
1295kJ (309 cal); 9.9g carbohydrate; 9.5g protein; 5.3g fibre

Risotto-filled zucchini flowers

2 cups (500ml) chicken stock
½ cup (125ml) dry white wine
pinch saffron
45g (1½ ounces) butter
1 small brown onion (80g), chopped finely
1 clove garlic, crushed
1 cup (200g) arborio rice
⅓ cup (25g) finely grated parmesan cheese
1 teaspoon finely grated lemon rind
2 tablespoons finely chopped fresh flat-leaf parsley
28 zucchini flowers with stem attached (420g)
cooking-oil spray

1 Combine stock, wine and saffron in medium saucepan; bring to the boil. Reduce heat; simmer, covered.
2 Meanwhile, melt butter in medium saucepan; cook onion and garlic, stirring, until onion softens. Add rice; stir over medium heat until rice is coated in butter mixture. Stir in ½ cup of the simmering stock mixture; cook, stirring, over low heat until liquid is absorbed. Continue adding stock mixture, in ½ cup batches, stirring, until liquid is absorbed after each addition. Total cooking time should be about 35 minutes or until rice is tender. Stir in cheese, rind and parsley, cover; cool 30 minutes.
3 Preheat oven to 200°C/400°F. Grease two oven trays.
4 Discard stamens from zucchini flowers; fill flowers with 1 level tablespoon of risotto mixture, twist petal tops to enclose filling.
5 Place zucchini flowers on trays; spray all over with cooking-oil spray. Roast, uncovered, about 15 minutes or until zucchini stems are tender.

prep + cook time 1 hour 30 minutes (+ cooling) **makes** 28
nutritional count per flower 1.8g total fat (1g saturated fat); 209kJ (50 cal); 6.2g carbohydrate; 1.3g protein; 0.4g fibre

Stuffed baby capsicums

24 vine sweet minicap baby capsicums (bell peppers) (350g)
250g (8 ounces) ricotta cheese
2 tablespoons finely grated parmesan cheese
2 tablespoons coarsely chopped roasted pine nuts
4 slices hot salami (40g), chopped finely
2 tablespoons finely chopped fresh oregano

1 Preheat oven to 200°C/400°F.
2 Carefully cut tops from capsicums; reserve tops. Scoop out and discard seeds and membranes.
3 Combine remaining ingredients in small bowl. Place mixture in medium piping bag fitted with 1cm (½-inch) plain tube. Pipe filling into capsicums; replace tops. Place capsicums, in single layer, in oiled medium shallow baking dish.
4 Roast capsicums about 20 minutes or until tender.

prep + cook time 1 hour **makes** 24
nutritional count per capsicum 2.6g total fat (1g saturated fat);
138kJ (33 cal); 0.5g carbohydrate; 1.9g protein; 0.2g fibre

Smoked chicken, radicchio and basil salad

340g (11 ounces) asparagus, trimmed, chopped coarsely
500g (1 pound) smoked chicken breast fillets, sliced thickly
2 medium radicchio (400g), trimmed, leaves torn
⅔ cup loosely packed fresh basil leaves
pesto dressing
2 teaspoons basil pesto
¼ cup (60ml) balsamic vinegar
¼ cup (60ml) olive oil

1 Boil, steam or microwave asparagus until tender; drain. Rinse under cold water; drain.
2 Meanwhile, make pesto dressing.
3 Place asparagus and dressing in large bowl with remaining ingredients; toss gently to combine.
pesto dressing Place ingredients in screw-top jar; shake well.

prep + cook time 15 minutes **serves** 4
nutritional count per serving 23.8g total fat (4.6g saturated fat); 1513kJ (362 cal); 2g carbohydrate; 33.8g protein; 3.2g fibre

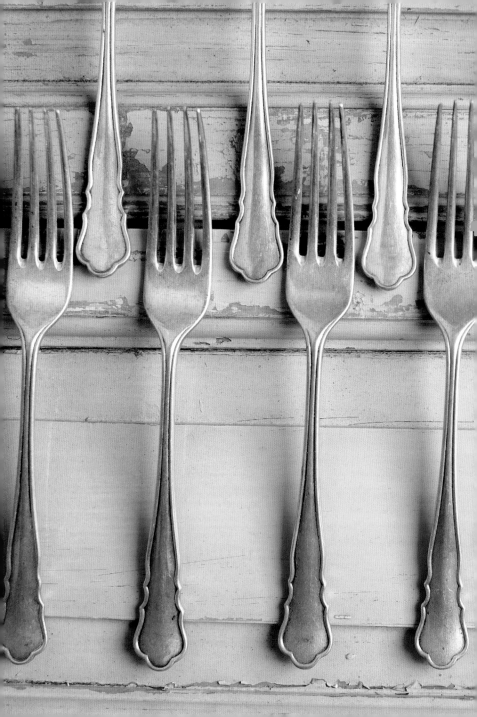

Mains

SEAFOOD

Octopus braised in red wine

⅓ cup (80ml) olive oil
625g (1¼ pounds) baby onions, halved
4 cloves garlic, crushed
1.5kg (3 pounds) cleaned baby octopus, halved
1½ cups (375ml) dry red wine
⅓ cup (95g) tomato paste
⅓ cup (80ml) red wine vinegar
3 large tomatoes (660g), peeled, seeded, chopped coarsely
2 bay leaves
1 fresh long red chilli, chopped finely
10 drained anchovy fillets (30g), chopped coarsely
⅓ cup finely chopped fresh oregano
1 cup coarsely chopped fresh flat-leaf parsley

1 Heat oil in large saucepan; cook onion and garlic, stirring, until onion softens. Add octopus; cook, stirring, until just changed in colour.
2 Add wine; cook, stirring, about 5 minutes or until pan liquid is reduced by about a third. Add tomato paste, vinegar, tomato, bay leaves, chilli and anchovies; bring to the boil. Reduce heat; simmer, covered, 1 hour. Uncover; simmer about 30 minutes or until sauce thickens and octopus is tender.
3 Stir in oregano and parsley off the heat; serve with thick slices of toasted ciabatta bread, if you like.

prep + cook time 2 hours **serves** 6
nutritional count per serving 14.7g total fat (1.8g saturated fat); 1593kJ (381 cal); 5.6g carbohydrate; 44.9g protein; 2.8g fibre

Cioppino

2 teaspoons olive oil
1 medium brown onion (150g), chopped coarsely
1 baby fennel bulb (130g), trimmed, chopped coarsely
3 cloves garlic, crushed
6 medium tomatoes (1kg), chopped coarsely
410g (13 ounces) canned crushed tomatoes
½ cup (125ml) dry white wine
1½ cups (375ml) fish stock
2 cooked blue swimmer crabs (700g)
500g (1 pound) uncooked large king prawns (shrimp)
450g (14 ounces) swordfish steaks
400g (13 ounces) clams, rinsed
150g (5 ounces) scallops
¼ cup coarsely chopped fresh basil
½ cup coarsely chopped fresh flat-leaf parsley

1 Heat oil in large saucepan; cook onion, fennel and garlic, stirring, until onion softens. Add fresh tomato; cook, stirring, about 5 minutes or until pulpy. Stir in undrained crushed tomatoes, wine and stock; reduce heat, simmer, covered, 20 minutes.
2 Meanwhile, remove back shell from crabs; discard grey gills. Rinse crab; using sharp knife, chop each crab into four pieces. Shell and devein prawns, leaving tails intact. Chop fish into 2cm (¾-inch) pieces.
3 Add clams to pan; simmer, covered, about 5 minutes or until clams open (discard any that do not). Add remaining seafood; cook, stirring occasionally, about 5 minutes or until seafood has changed in colour and is cooked as desired. Remove from heat; stir in herbs.

prep + cook time 45 minutes **serves** 4
nutritional count per serving 6.4g total fat (1.4g saturated fat);
1476kJ (352 cal); 13.1g carbohydrate; 54.2g protein; 5.9g fibre

Seafood stew

2 baby fennel bulbs (260g)
2 tablespoons lemon juice
1 tablespoon olive oil
2 medium brown onions (300g),
  chopped finely
4 cloves garlic, crushed
1 orange
⅓ cup (80ml) dry white wine
1 teaspoon chilli flakes
pinch saffron threads
800g (28 ounces) canned
  diced tomatoes
1 litre (4 cups) fish stock

1 teaspoon white sugar
750g (1½ pounds) uncooked
  medium king prawns (shrimp)
750g (1½ pounds) small
  black mussels
750g (1½ pounds) skinless
  white fish fillets, cut into
  3cm (1¼-inch) pieces
garlic croûtons
675g (1¼ pounds) loaf sourdough
  bread, sliced thickly
3 cloves garlic, halved
2 tablespoons olive oil

1 Trim fennel; reserve feathery fronds. Slice fennel as thinly as possible; combine with lemon juice in small bowl.

2 Heat oil in large saucepan; cook onion, stirring, until soft. Add garlic; cook, stirring, 1 minute.

3 Peel 3 thin strips of rind from orange. Stir rind, wine, chilli and saffron into onion mixture; cook, stirring, 2 minutes. Add undrained tomatoes; simmer, uncovered, about 10 minutes or until mixture thickens slightly. Add stock; simmer, uncovered, about 20 minutes or until liquid is reduced by about a quarter. Stir in sugar.

4 Shell and devein prawns. Scrub mussels, remove beards.

5 Add prawns, mussels and fish to tomato mixture. Cover; simmer, stirring occasionally, about 5 minutes or until prawns change in colour and mussels open (discard any that do not).

6 Meanwhile, make garlic croûtons.

7 Serve stew topped with fennel mixture and reserved fennel fronds; accompany with garlic croûtons.

garlic croûtons Toast bread both sides on heated grill plate (or grill or grill pan); rub one side of toast with cut garlic clove, drizzle with oil.

prep + cook time 1 hour **serves** 6
nutritional count per serving 17.2g total fat (3.5g saturated fat);
2792kJ (668 cal); 63.7g carbohydrate; 56.9g protein; 9.2g fibre

Swordfish with celery and bean salad

2 stalks celery (300g), trimmed, halved, sliced thinly
300g (9 ounces) canned cannellini beans, rinsed, drained
¼ cup coarsely chopped young celery leaves
4 swordfish steaks (700g)
dressing
⅓ cup (80ml) lemon juice
2 cloves garlic, chopped finely
¼ teaspoon salt
¼ teaspoon cracked black pepper
⅓ cup (80ml) extra virgin olive oil
1 tablespoon fresh oregano leaves, torn
1 tablespoon drained baby capers, rinsed

1 Make dressing.
2 Place celery, beans and celery leaves in small bowl with ¼ cup of the dressing; toss gently to combine.
3 Heat oiled large frying pan; cook fish until browned on both sides and cooked as desired. Remove from pan.
4 Add remaining dressing to same pan; bring to the boil.
5 Divide celery and bean salad among serving plates; top with fish, drizzle with warm dressing.
dressing Whisk juice, garlic, salt, pepper and oil in small bowl until thickened slighty. Stir in oregano and capers.

prep + cook time 25 minutes **serves** 4
nutritional count per serving 22.3g total fat (3.9g saturated fat); 1526kJ (365 cal); 2.8g carbohydrate; 37.4g protein; 2.3g fibre

Kingfish with salsa verde and white bean puree

1 tablespoon olive oil
1 clove garlic, crushed
1 medium brown onion (150g), chopped finely
3 x 400g (13 ounces) canned white beans, rinsed, drained
1 cup (250ml) chicken stock
¼ cup (60ml) pouring cream
4 kingfish fillets (800g), skin-on

salsa verde
½ cup finely chopped fresh flat-leaf parsley
¼ cup finely chopped fresh mint
¼ cup finely chopped fresh dill
¼ cup finely chopped fresh chives
1 tablespoon wholegrain mustard
2 tablespoons lemon juice
2 tablespoons drained baby capers, rinsed, chopped finely
1 clove garlic, crushed
¼ cup (60ml) olive oil

1 Make salsa verde.
2 Heat oil in medium saucepan; cook garlic and onion, stirring, until onion softens. Add beans and stock; bring to the boil. Reduce heat; simmer, uncovered, until almost all liquid has evaporated. Stir in cream; blend or process bean mixture until smooth.
3 Meanwhile, cook fish, skin-side down, in large heated oiled frying pan until cooked as desired.
4 Serve fish on white bean puree, topped with salsa verde.
salsa verde Combine ingredients in small bowl.

prep + cook time 50 minutes **serves** 4
nutritional count per serving 23.5g total fat (4.4g saturated fat); 1789kJ (428 cal); 7.4g carbohydrate; 46.9g protein; 5.6g fibre

Barbecued snapper with vegetable parcels

1 whole snapper (2kg)
1 clove garlic, sliced thinly
3 sprigs fresh rosemary
1 medium lemon (140g), sliced
45g (1½ ounces) butter
2 large zucchini (300g)
2 trimmed corn cobs (500g), sliced thickly
2 medium red capsicums (bell pepper) (400g), sliced thickly
1 large red onion (300g), cut into wedges

lemon herb butter
150g (5 ounces) butter, softened
1 clove garlic, crushed
2 teaspoons finely grated lemon rind
2 teaspoons finely chopped fresh rosemary

1 Make lemon herb butter.
2 Meanwhile, place fish on board; score fish both sides through thickest part of flesh. Push garlic and rosemary into cuts; fill cavity with one-third of the lemon slices.
3 Place a long piece of baking paper on bench; top with half the remaining lemon slices. Place fish on lemon; top with remaining lemon slices and butter. Fold paper over fish to completely enclose; wrap tightly in foil.
4 Cook fish on heated oiled grill plate (or grill or barbecue) 20 minutes; turn, cook further 20 minutes.
5 Meanwhile, cut zucchini in half crossways; cut each half lengthways into six. Combine zucchini with remaining ingredients in large bowl. Place eight 30cm (12-inch) foil squares on bench; divide vegetable mixture among foil squares. Gather corners of squares together; fold to completely enclose vegetables.
6 Cook vegetable parcels on heated oiled flat plate until vegetables are tender. Open parcels; top with slices of lemon herb butter. Serve with fish.
lemon herb butter Combine ingredients in small bowl. Place on piece of plastic wrap; shape into 6cm (2½-inch) log, wrap tightly. Freeze until firm; cut into eight slices.

prep + cook time 1 hour **serves** 8
nutritional count per serving 24.2g total fat (14.5g saturated fat); 1664kJ (398 cal); 12.4g carbohydrate; 30.9g protein; 4.2g fibre

Crisp-skinned ocean trout with bavette

375g (12 ounce) bavette pasta
¼ cup (60ml) vegetable oil
¼ cup loosely packed fresh sage leaves
¼ cup (50g) drained capers, rinsed
6 green onions (scallions), cut into 5cm (2-inch) lengths
4 ocean trout fillets (880g), skin-on
⅓ cup (80ml) lemon juice
1 tablespoon sweet chilli sauce
2 cloves garlic, crushed

1 Cook pasta in large saucepan of boiling water until just tender; drain.
2 Meanwhile, heat oil in large non-stick frying pan; shallow-fry sage, capers and onion, separately, until crisp.
3 Cook fish, skin-side up, on heated oiled grill plate (or grill or grill pan) until crisp both sides and cooked as desired.
4 Meanwhile, place pasta in large bowl with juice, chilli sauce, garlic and half the sage, half the capers and half the onion; toss gently to combine.
5 Divide pasta mixture among serving plates; top with fish, sprinkle with remaining sage, remaining capers and remaining onion.

prep + cook time 30 minutes **serves** 4
nutritional count per serving 18.3g total fat (3g saturated fat);
2784kJ (666 cal); 70g carbohydrate; 53.3g protein; 5.5g fibre

Prawn and asparagus risotto

500g (1 pound) uncooked medium king prawns (shrimp)
3 cups (750ml) chicken stock
3 cups (750ml) water
15g (½ ounce) butter
1 tablespoon olive oil
1 small brown onion (80g), chopped finely
2 cups (400g) arborio rice
½ cup (125ml) dry sherry
15g (½ ounce) butter, extra
2 teaspoons olive oil, extra
2 cloves garlic, crushed
500g (1 pound) asparagus, chopped coarsely
⅓ cup (25g) coarsely grated parmesan cheese
⅓ cup coarsely chopped fresh basil

1 Shell and devein prawns; chop prawn meat coarsely.
2 Place stock and the water in large saucepan; bring to the boil.
Reduce heat; simmer, covered.
3 Heat butter and oil in large saucepan; cook onion, stirring, until soft.
Add rice; stir to coat rice in onion mixture. Add sherry; cook, stirring,
until liquid is almost evaporated. Stir in 1 cup simmering stock mixture;
cook, stirring, over low heat until liquid is absorbed. Continue adding stock
mixture, in 1-cup batches, stirring, until absorbed after each addition.
Total cooking time should be about 35 minutes or until rice is tender.
4 Heat extra butter and extra oil in medium frying pan; cook prawn
meat and garlic, stirring, until prawn just changes colour.
5 Boil, steam or microwave asparagus until just tender; drain.
6 Add asparagus, prawn mixture and cheese to risotto; cook, stirring,
until cheese melts. Stir in basil.

prep + cook time 1 hour 10 minutes **serves** 4
nutritional count per serving 14.7g total fat (5.5g saturated fat);
2516kJ (602 cal); 82.8g carbohydrate; 26.3g protein; 2.6g fibre

Seafood risotto

1.5 litres (6 cups) chicken stock
2 cups (500ml) water
2 tablespoons olive oil
1 medium leek (350g), sliced thinly
1 fresh small red thai chilli, chopped finely
3 cups (600g) arborio rice
pinch saffron threads
1 cup (250ml) dry white wine
2 tablespoons tomato paste
1.5kg (3 pounds) marinara mix
1 cup (120g) frozen peas
2 teaspoons finely grated lemon rind
1 cup loosely packed fresh flat-leaf parsley leaves

1 Place stock and the water in large saucepan; bring to the boil.
Reduce heat; simmer, covered.
2 Heat oil in large saucepan; cook leek and chilli, stirring, until leek
softens. Add rice and saffron; stir to coat rice in leek mixture. Add
wine and paste; cook, stirring, until wine has almost evaporated.
Stir in ½ cup simmering stock mixture; cook, stirring, over low heat until
liquid is absorbed. Continue adding stock mixture, in ½-cup batches,
stirring, until absorbed after each addition. Total cooking time should
be about 30 minutes.
3 Add marinara mix and peas; mix gently. Simmer, covered, 5 minutes.
Uncover; simmer until all stock has been absorbed and seafood is tender.
Stir in rind and parsley.

prep + cook time 1 hour 15 minutes **serves** 8
nutritional count per serving 5.9g total fat (1.1g saturated fat);
1547kJ (370 cal); 63.2g carbohydrate; 8.9g protein; 2.9g fibre

Slow-roasted pesto salmon

1 cup loosely packed fresh basil leaves
2 cloves garlic, chopped coarsely
2 tablespoons roasted pine nuts
2 tablespoons lemon juice
¼ cup (60ml) olive oil
1.5kg (3 pound) piece salmon fillet, skin-on
2 tablespoons olive oil, extra
2 large red capsicums (bell pepper) (700g), chopped coarsely
1 large red onion (300g), chopped coarsely

1 Preheat oven to 160°C/325°F.
2 Blend or process basil, garlic, nuts and juice until combined.
With motor operating, gradually add oil in thin, steady stream until
pesto thickens slightly.
3 Place fish, skin-side down, on piece of oiled foil large enough to
completely enclose fish; coat fish with half of the pesto. Gather corners
of foil together above fish; twist to completely enclose fish. Place parcel
on oven tray; roast about 45 minutes or until cooked as desired.
4 Meanwhile, heat extra oil in large frying pan; cook capsicum and onion,
stirring, until onion softens.
5 Place fish parcel on serving platter, unwrap; top with onion mixture,
drizzle with remaining pesto.

prep + cook time 1 hour 10 minutes **serves** 8
nutritional count per serving 8.3g total fat (1.4g saturated fat);
543kJ (130 cal); 1.8g carbohydrate; 11.8g protein; 0.6g fibre

Fish fillets pan-fried with pancetta and caper herb butter

75g (2½ ounces) butter, softened
2 tablespoons coarsely chopped fresh flat-leaf parsley
1 tablespoon drained capers, rinsed
2 cloves garlic, quartered
2 green onions (scallions), chopped coarsely
8 slices pancetta (120g)
4 white fish fillets (600g)
1 tablespoon olive oil
345g (11 ounces) asparagus, trimmed

1 Blend or process butter, parsley, capers, garlic and onion until mixture forms a smooth paste.
2 Spread 1 heaped tablespoon of the butter mixture and two slices of the pancetta on each fish fillet.
3 Heat oil in large heavy-based frying pan; cook fish, pancetta-butter-side down, until pancetta is crisp. Turn fish carefully; cook, uncovered, until cooked as desired.
4 Meanwhile, boil, steam or microwave asparagus until tender.
5 Serve fish and asparagus drizzled with pan juices.

prep + cook time 25 minutes **serves** 4
nutritional count per serving 27.5g total fat (13.4g saturated fat); 1705kJ (408 cal); 1.8g carbohydrate; 38.2g protein; 1.4g fibre

Anchovy and garlic tuna with tomato and oregano

1kg (2-pound) tuna fillet, trimmed, skinned
3 cloves garlic, sliced thinly
¼ cup firmly packed fresh oregano leaves
8 drained anchovy fillets, halved
¼ cup (60ml) olive oil
1 large brown onion (200g), sliced thinly
4 large egg (plum) tomatoes (360g), seeded, chopped coarsely
¼ cup (60ml) balsamic vinegar
2 tablespoons dry white wine
¼ cup (60ml) fish stock
1 tablespoon drained baby capers, rinsed
¼ cup coarsely chopped fresh basil

1 Preheat oven to 200°C/400°F.
2 Using sharp knife, make 16 cuts in tuna; press 16 slices of the garlic, 16 oregano leaves and anchovy halves into cuts.
3 Heat 2 tablespoons of the oil in deep medium flameproof baking dish; cook tuna, uncovered, until browned. Remove from dish.
4 Heat remaining oil in same dish; cook onion, stirring, until soft. Combine tomato, vinegar, wine, stock, remaining garlic and remaining oregano in dish then add tuna; bring to the boil. Cook, uncovered, in oven about 10 minutes or until tuna is cooked as desired. Remove tuna from dish; slice thinly. Stir capers and basil into sauce.
5 Serve tuna with sauce and mashed potato, if you like.

prep + cook time 45 minutes **serves** 4
nutritional count per serving 28.7g total fat (7.8g saturated fat); 2286kJ (547 cal); 4.1g carbohydrate; 65.8g protein; 1.6g fibre

POULTRY

Chicken cacciatore

2 tablespoons olive oil
1.5kg (3 pounds) chicken thigh cutlets, skin on
1 medium brown onion (150g), chopped finely
1 clove garlic, crushed
½ cup (125ml) dry white wine
2 tablespoons white wine vinegar
½ cup (125ml) chicken stock
410g (13 ounces) canned crushed tomatoes
¼ cup (70g) tomato paste
2 drained anchovy fillets, chopped finely
½ cup (60g) seeded black olives, chopped coarsely
½ cup coarsely chopped fresh flat-leaf parsley

1 Heat half the oil in large saucepan; cook chicken, in batches, until browned all over. Remove from pan.
2 Heat remaining oil in same pan; cook onion and garlic, stirring, until onion softens. Stir in wine, vinegar, stock, undrained tomatoes, paste and anchovies.
3 Return chicken to pan, fitting pieces tightly together in a single layer; bring to the boil. Reduce heat; simmer, covered, 20 minutes. Uncover; simmer about 30 minutes or until chicken is tender and sauce is reduced. Skim fat from surface; stir in olives and parsley.

prep + cook time 1 hours 30 minutes **serves** 4
nutritional count per serving 39.9g total fat (10.8g saturated fat); 2454kJ (587 cal); 10.8g carbohydrate; 40.5g protein; 3.1g fibre

Chicken stuffed with ricotta, basil and prosciutto

8 chicken thigh cutlets (1.3kg)
⅔ cup (130g) ricotta cheese
4 slices prosciutto (60g), halved lengthways
8 large fresh basil leaves
1 tablespoon olive oil
1 medium brown onion (150g), chopped finely
1 medium carrot (120g), chopped finely
1 stalk celery (150g), trimmed, chopped finely
2 cloves garlic, chopped finely
2 tablespoons tomato paste
½ cup (125ml) dry white wine
8 small tomatoes (720g), peeled, chopped coarsely
410g (13 ounces) canned diced tomatoes
½ cup (125ml) water

1 Using small sharp knife, cut a pocket through thickest part of each cutlet over the bone. Push 1 tablespoon of the cheese, one slice of prosciutto and 1 basil leaf into each pocket; secure pocket closed with toothpick.
2 Heat oil in large deep flameproof baking dish; cook chicken, in batches, until browned all over. Remove from pan.
3 Preheat oven to 160°C/325°F.
4 Cook onion, carrot, celery and garlic in same dish, stirring, about 5 minutes or until onion softens. Add paste; cook, stirring, 2 minutes. Add wine; bring to the boil. Reduce heat; simmer, uncovered, 1 minute. Add chopped tomato, undrained diced tomatoes and the water; bring to the boil. Reduce heat; simmer, uncovered, 10 minutes.
5 Return chicken to dish, cover; cook in oven 1 hour. Uncover; cook further 20 minutes or until chicken is cooked through. Remove toothpicks before serving.

prep + cook time 2 hours 30 minutes **serves** 4
nutritional count per serving 33g total fat (10.5g saturated fat); 2746kJ (657 cal); 12.2g carbohydrate; 70.6g protein; 5.8g fibre

Pollo parmigiana-style

2 chicken breast fillets (400g)
2 tablespoons plain (all-purpose) flour
1 egg
1 tablespoon milk
1 cup (70g) stale breadcrumbs
¼ cup (60ml) vegetable oil
⅓ cup (85g) bottled tomato pasta sauce, warmed
4 slices leg ham (185g)
125g (4 ounces) gruyère cheese, grated coarsely

1 Preheat grill (broiler).
2 Split chicken fillets in half horizontally. Toss chicken in flour;
shake away excess. Dip chicken pieces, one at a time, in combined
egg and milk, then in breadcrumbs.
3 Heat oil in large frying pan; shallow-fry chicken, in batches,
until browned and cooked through. Remove from pan; drain on
absorbent paper.
4 Place chicken on oven tray; spoon pasta sauce over chicken,
then top with ham and cheese. Place under grill until cheese melts.
5 Serve with a parmesan and baby rocket (arugula) salad, if desired.

prep + cook time 30 minutes **serves** 4
nutritional count per serving 28.6g total fat (8.7g saturated fat);
2103kJ (503 cal); 17.9g carbohydrate; 43.3g protein; 1.3g fibre

Chicken margherita

500g (1 pound) baby vine-ripened truss tomatoes
4 chicken breast fillets (800g)
⅓ cup (90g) basil pesto
185g (6 ounces) bocconcini cheese, sliced thinly
20g (¾ ounce) baby spinach leaves
8 slices prosciutto (120g)

1 Preheat oven to 220°C/425°F.
2 Remove four tomatoes from truss; slice thinly.
3 Split one chicken fillet in half horizontally; open out. Spread one tablespoon of pesto on one side of chicken fillet; top with one-quarter of the cheese, one-quarter of the sliced tomato and one-quarter of the spinach. Fold chicken fillet over filling; wrap with two slices prosciutto to enclose securely. Repeat process with remaining chicken, pesto, cheese, sliced tomato, spinach and prosciutto.
4 Roast chicken and remaining tomatoes in large oiled shallow baking dish about 20 minutes or until cooked through. Serve chicken sliced with roasted tomatoes.

prep + cook time 30 minutes **serves** 4
nutritional count per serving 28.7g total fat (10.5g saturated fat); 2144kJ (513 cal); 3g carbohydrate; 59.7g protein; 2.3g fibre

Chicken, pea, sage and prosciutto risotto

3 cups (750ml) chicken stock
3 cups (750ml) water
15g (½ ounce) butter
2 tablespoons olive oil
1 small brown onion (80g), chopped finely
2 cups (400g) arborio rice
½ cup (125ml) dry white wine
350g (11 ounces) chicken breast fillets, chopped coarsely
2 cloves garlic, crushed
1½ cups (180g) frozen peas
6 slices prosciutto (90g)
2 tablespoons finely shredded fresh sage

1 Place stock and the water in large saucepan; bring to the boil.
Reduce heat; simmer, covered.
2 Heat butter and half the oil in large saucepan; cook onion, stirring,
until soft. Add rice; stir rice to coat in mixture. Add wine; cook, stirring,
until liquid is almost evaporated.
3 Stir in 1 cup simmering stock mixture; cook, stirring, over low heat
until liquid is absorbed. Continue adding stock mixture, in 1-cup batches,
stirring, until absorbed after each addition. Total cooking time should be
about 35 minutes or until rice is tender.
4 Meanwhile, heat remaining oil in medium frying pan; cook chicken,
stirring, until cooked through. Add garlic; stir until fragrant. Stir chicken
mixture and peas into risotto.
5 Cook prosciutto in same frying pan until crisp; drain on absorbent
paper then break into coarse pieces. Stir sage and half of the prosciutto
into risotto; sprinkle remaining prosciutto over individual risotto servings.

prep + cook time 1 hour **serves** 4
nutritional count per serving 18.8g total fat (5.1g saturated fat);
2784kJ (666 cal); 84.1g carbohydrate; 24.5g protein; 3.9g fibre

Prosciutto-wrapped chickens with lemon and sage

8 small chickens (poussin) (3.2kg)
1 medium lemon (140g)
16 fresh sage leaves
8 thin slices prosciutto (120g)
2 medium lemons (280g), extra
fennel rub
1 teaspoon fennel seeds, toasted, crushed
1 clove garlic, crushed
2 tablespoons olive oil

1 Preheat oven to 220°C/425°F.
2 Wash chickens under cold water; clean cavity well. Pat dry inside and out with absorbent paper.
3 Cut lemon into eight wedges. Place a lemon wedge and 2 sage leaves into each chicken cavity.
4 Make fennel rub; rub mixture all over chickens.
5 Wrap a slice of prosciutto around centre of each chicken; secure with a toothpick. Divide chickens between two baking dishes.
6 Roast chickens about 45 minutes or until browned and cooked through. Transfer to a serving platter; cover with foil, stand 15 minutes.
7 Remove toothpicks before serving with extra lemon wedges, if you like.
fennel rub Combine ingredients in small bowl.

prep + cook time 1 hour 10 minutes **serves** 8
nutritional count per serving 44.9g total fat (13.3g saturated fat); 2546kJ (609 cal); 0.3g carbohydrate; 51.8g protein; 0.3g fibre
tip Remove toothpicks before serving.

Spinach and ricotta-stuffed chicken parmigiana

8 chicken schnitzels (800g)
45g (1½ ounces) baby spinach leaves
1⅓ cups (320g) ricotta cheese
¼ cup (35g) plain (all-purpose) flour
2 eggs
2 tablespoons milk
1½ cups (105g) stale breadcrumbs
vegetable oil, for shallow-frying
1 cup (260g) bottled tomato pasta sauce
1 cup (100g) coarsely grated mozzarella cheese

1 Preheat oven to 200°C/400°F.
2 Top each schnitzel with spinach and cheese, leaving 1cm (½-inch) border around edges. Fold in half to secure filling; press down firmly.
3 Coat schnitzels in flour; shake off excess. Dip in combined egg and milk, then in breadcrumbs.
4 Heat oil in large frying pan; cook schnitzels, in batches, until browned and cooked through. Remove from pan; drain on absorbent paper.
5 Place schnitzels in oiled shallow large baking dish; top with sauce and cheese. Bake about 10 minutes or until cheese melts.

prep + cook time 35 minutes **serves** 4
nutritional count per serving 40.2g total fat (15.3g saturated fat);
3194kJ (764 cal); 31.9g carbohydrate; 67.2g protein; 2.9g fibre

Mini meatloaves Italian-style

500g (1 pound) minced (ground) chicken
2 cloves garlic, crushed
1 fresh small red thai chilli, chopped finely
⅓ cup (35g) packaged breadcrumbs
1 egg
⅓ cup coarsely chopped fresh basil
⅓ cup (50g) finely chopped sun-dried tomatoes in oil
2 tablespoons roasted pine nuts, chopped coarsely
cooking-oil spray
4 slices prosciutto (60g)

1 Combine mince, garlic, chilli, breadcrumbs, egg, basil, tomato and
nuts in large bowl; shape mixture into four meatloaves.
2 Coat four 25cm (10-inch) pieces foil with cooking-oil spray.
Wrap a slice of prosciutto around each meatloaf; wrap loaves in foil.
3 Cook meatloaves on heated oiled grill plate (or grill or grill pan),
turning occasionally, about 25 minutes or until cooked through.
Remove foil; serve sliced meatloaves with potato salad, if you like.

prep + cook time 45 minutes **serves** 4
nutritional count per serving 19.3g total fat (7.2g saturated fat);
1467kJ (351 cal); 10.8g carbohydrate; 32.1g protein; 2.9g fibre

Chicken with creamy pancetta, pea and tarragon sauce

2 tablespoons olive oil
8 chicken drumsticks (1.2kg)
2 shallots (50g), chopped finely
1 clove garlic, crushed
100g (3 ounces) sliced pancetta, shredded finely
½ cup (125ml) dry white wine
1¼ cups (310ml) pouring cream
½ cup (60g) frozen peas
1 tablespoon coarsely chopped fresh tarragon

1 Heat half the oil in large frying pan; cook chicken, in batches, until cooked through. Remove from pan.
2 Heat remaining oil in same cleaned pan; cook shallots, garlic and pancetta, stirring, over medium heat until pancetta browns. Add wine; bring to the boil. Reduce heat; simmer, uncovered, about 2 minutes or until mixture reduces by half.
3 Add cream and peas; bring to the boil. Reduce heat; simmer, uncovered, 4 minutes, stirring occasionally. Add tarragon and chicken; simmer, uncovered, 2 minutes.

prep + cook time 50 minutes **serves** 4
nutritional count per serving 78.7g total fat (35.2g saturated fat); 3904kJ (934 cal); 3.7g carbohydrate; 49.7g protein; 1.1g fibre
tip You can use a 300ml carton of cream without affecting the recipe.

Balsamic chicken with eggplant puree

8 chicken drumsticks (1.2kg)
2 tablespoons balsamic vinegar
2 tablespoons light brown sugar
1 large eggplant (500g), halved lengthways
6 medium egg (plum) tomatoes (450g), halved

1 Preheat oven to 240°C/475°F.
2 Combine chicken, vinegar and sugar in large shallow baking dish. Roast, covered, 15 minutes.
3 Meanwhile, pierce eggplant all over with fork; place, cut-side down, on oiled oven tray. Roast, uncovered, about 15 minutes or until tender. When cool enough to handle, peel eggplant; blend or process eggplant until smooth.
4 Uncover chicken; add tomatoes to dish. Roast, uncovered, about 15 minutes or until chicken is cooked through.
5 Serve chicken with eggplant puree and tomatoes; drizzle with pan juices.

prep + cook time 35 minutes **serves** 4
nutritional count per serving 21.4g total fat (6.3g saturated fat); 1643kJ (393 cal); 12.2g carbohydrate; 36g protein; 4.5g fibre

Gorgonzola and sage-stuffed chicken

⅓ cup (50g) semi-dried tomatoes in oil
4 chicken breast fillets (800g)
125g (4 ounces) gorgonzola cheese, cut into four slices
12 fresh sage leaves
8 slices pancetta (120g)
75g (2½ ounces) baby rocket (arugula) leaves

1 Drain tomatoes; reserve 2 tablespoons of the oil.
2 Cut horizontal slits into chicken fillets, three-quarters of the way through, to make pockets.
3 Divide cheese, sage and tomatoes among pockets in chicken; wrap two slices of pancetta around each chicken breast.
4 Cook chicken in heated oiled large frying pan until cooked through.
5 Toss rocket with reserved oil; serve with thickly sliced chicken.

prep + cook time 35 minutes **serves** 4
nutritional count per serving 24.3g total fat (10.3g saturated fat); 1940kJ (464 cal); 4.8g carbohydrate; 55.5g protein; 2.1g fibre

Chicken, spinach and ricotta bake

You need half a large barbecued chicken (450g) for this recipe.

1 tablespoon olive oil
1 large brown onion (200g), chopped finely
2 cloves garlic, crushed
10 instant lasagne sheets (200g)
1½ cups (240g) shredded barbecue chicken meat
1 cup (100g) coarsely grated pizza cheese
3 cups (750ml) bottled tomato pasta sauce
2 cups (500ml) water
½ cup (120g) firm ricotta cheese, crumbled
60g (2 ounces) baby spinach leaves

1 Heat oil in shallow flameproof dish; cook onion and garlic, stirring, until onion softens.
2 Break lasagne sheets into bite-sized pieces; scatter over onion mixture, then top with chicken and half the pizza cheese. Pour combined pasta sauce and the water over the top; simmer, covered, about 20 minutes or until pasta is tender.
3 Meanwhile, preheat grill (broiler).
4 Sprinkle bake with ricotta and remaining pizza cheese; place under grill about 5 minutes or until cheese melts. Stand, covered, 10 minutes; top with spinach just before serving.

prep + cook time 50 minutes **serves** 4
nutritional count per serving 18.8g total fat (7.7g saturated fat); 2195kJ (525 cal); 49.7g carbohydrate; 34.9g protein; 6.9g fibre

Duck, pear and blue cheese salad

4 duck breast fillets (600g)
1 small red oak lettuce, trimmed
2 witlof (belgian endive) (250g), trimmed
1 medium pear (230g), halved, cored, sliced thinly
1 cup (100g) roasted walnuts
150g (5 ounces) soft blue cheese, crumbled
red wine vinaigrette
¼ cup (60ml) olive oil
¼ cup (60ml) red wine vinegar
2 teaspoons wholegrain mustard

1 Cook duck, skin-side down, in heated large frying pan about 5 minutes or until skin is browned and crisp. Turn duck; cook about 5 minutes or until cooked as desired. Drain on absorbent paper; slice thinly.
2 Meanwhile, make red wine vinaigrette.
3 Place duck in large bowl with lettuce, witlof, pear and nuts; toss gently to combine. Drizzle salad with vinaigrette; sprinkle with cheese.
red wine vinaigrette Place ingredients in screw-top jar; shake well.

prep + cook time 30 minutes **serves** 4
nutritional count per serving 99g total fat (27.5g saturated fat);
4431kJ (1060 cal); 8.8g carbohydrate; 33.1g protein; 6.5g fibre

Roasted chickens with dill and walnut pesto

⅓ cup firmly packed fresh
   flat-leaf parsley leaves
½ cup firmly packed fresh
   dill sprigs
½ cup (50g) roasted walnuts,
   chopped coarsely
¼ cup (20g) finely grated
   parmesan cheese
¼ cup (60ml) lemon juice
¼ cup (60ml) olive oil
4 small chickens (poussin) (2kg)
2 medium lemons (280g),
   quartered

risoni salad
1 cup (220g) risoni pasta
6 slices pancetta (90g),
   chopped finely
⅓ cup (50g) roasted pine nuts
¼ cup finely chopped fresh basil
¼ cup finely chopped fresh
   flat-leaf parsley
2 tablespoons olive oil
1 tablespoon red wine vinegar

1 Preheat oven to 180°C/350°F.

2 Blend or process herbs, nuts, cheese and juice until combined. With motor operating, gradually add oil in thin, steady stream until pesto thickens slightly. Reserve 1 tablespoon of pesto for risoni salad.

3 Wash chickens under cold water; clean cavity well. Discard necks; pat dry inside and out with absorbent paper. Loosen skin; rub remaining pesto between skin and flesh and over outside of chickens. Place two lemon quarters into each chicken cavity.

4 Place chickens on oiled wire rack over baking dish; roast, uncovered, about 45 minutes or until cooked through.

5 Meanwhile, make risoni salad.

6 Remove chickens from baking dish; discard pan juices. Halve chickens lengthways; serve with salad.

risoni salad Cook pasta in large saucepan of boiling water until just tender; drain. Cook pancetta in small heated non-stick frying pan, stirring, about 5 minutes or until crisp. Place pasta and pancetta in large bowl with nuts, herbs, oil, vinegar and reserved pesto; toss gently to combine.

prep + cook time 1 hour 40 minutes **serves** 4
nutritional count per serving 85.1g total fat (18.9g saturated fat); 5029kJ (1203 cal); 40.3g carbohydrate; 65.5g protein; 5.5g fibre

Roasted quail with braised vegetables

8 quails (1.3kg)
8 slices prosciutto (120g)
15g (½ ounce) butter
½ cup (125ml) dry white wine
2 baby fennel bulbs (260g), trimmed, sliced thinly
4 cloves garlic, unpeeled
1 large red capsicum (bell pepper) (350g), sliced thinly
2 medium zucchini (240g), halved lengthways, sliced thickly
½ cup (125ml) chicken stock
1 medium lemon (140g), cut into eight wedges
¼ cup (60ml) pouring cream
1 tablespoon fresh oregano leaves

1 Preheat oven to 200°C/400°F.
2 Discard necks from quails. Wash quails under cold water; pat dry inside and out with absorbent paper. Tuck legs along body; wrap tightly with prosciutto to hold legs in place.
3 Heat butter in large flameproof baking dish; cook quails, in batches, until browned all over. Remove from dish.
4 Place wine in same dish; bring to the boil. Reduce heat; simmer, uncovered, until wine has reduced to 1 tablespoon. Add fennel, garlic, capsicum, zucchini and stock; return to the boil.
5 Place quails on top of vegetables; roast in oven 20 minutes. Add lemon; roast further 10 minutes or until quails are cooked through.
6 Remove quails and garlic from dish. When cool enough to handle, squeeze garlic from skins into dish; stir in cream and oregano.
Serve quails on vegetables.

prep + cook time 1 hour **serves** 4
nutritional count per serving 30.8g total fat (12.4g saturated fat); 2052kJ (491 cal); 6.9g carbohydrate; 39.1g protein; 4.2g fibre

BEEF & VEAL

Meatballs napoletana

500g (1 pound) minced (ground) beef
1 egg
½ cup (50g) packaged breadcrumbs
¼ cup (20g) finely grated parmesan cheese
¼ cup finely chopped fresh flat-leaf parsley
2 tablespoons olive oil
1 small brown onion (80g), chopped finely
1 clove garlic, crushed
2½ cups (625ml) bottled tomato pasta sauce
½ cup (60g) frozen peas
¼ cup coarsely chopped fresh basil

1 Combine mince, egg, breadcrumbs, cheese and parsley in medium bowl. Using wetted hands, roll level tablespoons of mince mixture into balls.
2 Heat half the oil in large frying pan; cook meatballs, in batches, until browned and cooked through. Remove from pan.
3 Heat remaining oil in same pan; cook onion and garlic, stirring, until onion softens. Add sauce; bring to the boil. Add meatballs, reduce heat; simmer, uncovered, about 10 minutes or until sauce thickens slightly. Add peas and basil; simmer, uncovered, until peas are tender.
4 Serve meatballs and sauce with crusty bread, if you like.

prep + cook time 1 hour **makes** 26
nutritional count per meatball 3.9g total fat (1.2g saturated fat); 305kJ (73 cal); 4.1g carbohydrate; 4.9g protein; 0.8g fibre

Tuscan beef stew

1 tablespoon olive oil
400g (13 ounces) spring onions, trimmed
1kg (2 pounds) chuck steak, cut into 3cm (1¼-inch) cubes
30g (1 ounce) butter
2 tablespoons plain (all-purpose) flour
2 cups (500ml) dry red wine
1 cup (250ml) beef stock
1 cup (250ml) water
2 cloves garlic, crushed
6 sprigs thyme
2 bay leaves
1 stalk celery (150g), trimmed, chopped coarsely
410g (13 ounces) baby carrots, trimmed, halved
2 cups (250g) frozen peas
⅓ cup coarsely chopped fresh flat-leaf parsley

1 Heat oil in large heavy-based saucepan; cook onions, stirring occasionally, about 10 minutes or until browned lightly, remove from pan.
2 Cook steak, in batches, over high heat in same pan, until browned all over. Remove from pan.
3 Melt butter in same saucepan, add flour; cook, stirring, until mixture bubbles and thickens. Gradually stir in wine, stock and the water; stir until mixture boils and thickens. Return steak to pan with garlic, thyme and bay leaves; bring to the boil. Reduce heat; simmer, covered, 1½ hours.
4 Add onions to pan with celery and carrot; simmer, covered, 30 minutes. Add peas; simmer, uncovered, until peas are just tender. Stir in parsley just before serving.

prep + cook time 2 hours 50 minutes **serves** 4
nutritional count per serving 22.7g total fat (9.5g saturated fat); 2529kJ (605 cal); 16.8g carbohydrate; 58.2g protein; 9g fibre

Grilled steaks with anchovy butter

6 new-york cut steaks (1.3kg)
2 tablespoons olive oil
lemony potato wedges
1.5kg (3 pounds) potatoes
¼ cup (60ml) olive oil
2 cloves garlic, crushed
1 tablespoon finely grated lemon rind
2 teaspoons sea salt flakes
anchovy butter
75g (2½ ounces) butter, softened
6 drained anchovy fillets, chopped coarsely
2 cloves garlic, crushed
2 tablespoons finely chopped fresh flat-leaf parsley

1 Make lemony potato wedges and anchovy butter.
2 About 10 minutes before wedges are cooked, brush beef all over with oil; cook on heated grill plate (or grill or grill pan) until cooked as desired. Cover beef; stand 5 minutes.
3 Serve beef topped with sliced anchovy butter and potato wedges.
lemony potato wedges Preheat oven to 220°C/425°F. Line oven tray with baking paper. Slice potatoes lengthways into 8 wedges; boil, steam or microwave until slightly softened. Drain; pat dry with absorbent paper. Combine potato in large bowl with oil, garlic, rind and salt. Place wedges, in single layer, on tray; roast about 50 minutes or until browned lightly.
anchovy butter Mash ingredients in small bowl with fork until well combined. Roll mixture tightly in plastic wrap to make a log; refrigerate until firm.

prep + cook time 1 hour **serves** 6
nutritional count per serving 39.8g total fat (14.9g saturated fat); 2989kJ (715 cal); 33.1g carbohydrate; 53.7g protein; 5.5g fibre

Veal cutlets with green olive salsa

2 tablespoons olive oil
2 cloves garlic, crushed
1 tablespoon finely chopped fresh oregano
2 teaspoons finely grated lemon rind
1 tablespoon lemon juice
4 veal cutlets (500g)
green olive salsa
1 tablespoon lemon juice
¼ cup coarsely chopped fresh flat-leaf parsley
½ cup (80g) finely chopped large green olives
1 small green capsicum (bell pepper) (150g), chopped finely
1 tablespoon olive oil
1 clove garlic, crushed
1 tablespoon finely chopped fresh oregano

1 Make green olive salsa.
2 Combine oil, garlic, oregano, rind and juice in small bowl; brush mixture over veal.
3 Cook veal on heated oiled grill plate (or grill or grill pan) until browned both sides and cooked as desired.
4 Serve veal with salsa and barbecued kipfler potatoes, if you like.
green olive salsa Combine ingredients in small bowl.

prep + cook time 35 minutes **serves** 4
nutritional count per serving 16.3g total fat (2.7g saturated fat); 1112kJ (266 cal); 5.8g carbohydrate; 23.4g protein; 1.2g fibre

Balsamic rosemary grilled veal

2 tablespoons olive oil
2 tablespoons balsamic vinegar
1 tablespoon fresh rosemary leaves
2 cloves garlic, crushed
4 veal steaks (500g)
4 medium egg (plum) tomatoes (300g), halved
4 flat mushrooms (320g)

1 Combine oil, vinegar, rosemary, garlic and veal in medium bowl.
2 Cook veal on heated oiled grill plate (or grill or grill pan), brushing occasionally with vinegar mixture, until cooked as desired. Remove from heat; cover to keep warm.
3 Cook tomato and mushrooms on heated oiled grill plate until tender. Serve veal with grilled vegetables.

prep + cook time 25 minutes **serves** 4
nutritional count per serving 11.3g total fat (1.8g saturated fat); 1016kJ (243 cal); 2.1g carbohydrate; 31.6g protein; 3.3g fibre

Spicy veal pizzaiola

2 tablespoons olive oil
2 cloves garlic, crushed
4 slices pancetta (60g), chopped finely
¼ cup (60ml) dry white wine
2½ cups (625ml) bottled tomato pasta sauce
1 teaspoon dried chilli flakes
4 veal cutlets (680g)
75g (2½ ounces) baby spinach leaves

1 Heat 2 teaspoons of the oil in large saucepan; cook garlic and pancetta, stirring, about 5 minutes. Add wine; cook, stirring, until wine is reduced by half. Add sauce and chilli; simmer, uncovered, about 15 minutes or until sauce thickens.
2 Meanwhile, heat remaining oil in large frying pan; cook veal, in batches, until cooked as desired. Remove from pan.
3 Remove sauce from heat; stir in spinach. Top veal with sauce.

prep + cook time 30 minutes **serves** 4
nutritional count per serving 14.6g total fat (2.8g saturated fat); 1555kJ (372 cal); 18.8g carbohydrate; 36.3g protein; 4.3g fibre

Veal and asparagus with basil mayo

4 veal cutlets (680g)
16 fresh basil leaves
4 slices prosciutto (60g)
345g (11 ounces) asparagus, trimmed
1 tablespoon olive oil
basil mayonnaise
½ cup (150g) mayonnaise
⅓ cup lightly packed fresh basil leaves
1 tablespoon lemon juice

1 Preheat oven to 200°C/400°F. Oil two oven trays.
2 Place cutlets on one tray; top with basil and prosciutto (secure with toothpick, if necessary). Roast 20 minutes or until cutlets are cooked as desired.
3 Place asparagus on remaining tray, drizzle with oil; roast for last 10 minutes of cutlet cooking time.
4 Meanwhile, make basil mayonnaise.
5 Serve cutlets with asparagus and mayonnaise.
basil mayonnaise Blend or process ingredients until smooth.

prep + cook time 30 minutes **serves** 4
nutritional count per serving 20.8g total fat (3.3g saturated fat); 1522kJ (364 cal); 8.5g carbohydrate; 35.3g protein; 1.2g fibre

Venetian calves liver and onions

2 cups (500ml) water
2 cups (500ml) milk
1 cup (170g) polenta
½ cup (40g) finely grated parmesan cheese
½ cup (125ml) pouring cream
¼ cup coarsely chopped fresh flat-leaf parsley
45g (1 ½ ounces) butter
2 tablespoons olive oil
3 medium brown onions (450g), sliced thinly
2 teaspoons cornflour (cornstarch)
¾ cup (180ml) beef stock
2 teaspoons dijon mustard
500g (1 pound) calves liver, sliced thinly
½ teaspoon balsamic vinegar

1 Bring the water and milk to the boil in large saucepan. Add polenta in a slow, steady stream, stirring constantly. Reduce heat; simmer, stirring occasionally, about 20 minutes or until polenta thickens. Stir in cheese, cream and parsley. Cover to keep warm.
2 Meanwhile, heat butter and half the oil in large frying pan; cook onion, stirring, until onion softens. Stir in blended cornflour, stock and mustard; cook, stirring, until sauce boils and thickens.
3 Heat remaining oil in another large frying pan; cook liver quickly over high heat until browned both sides and cooked as desired.
4 Divide polenta among serving dishes, top with liver. Just before serving, stir vinegar into sauce; spoon onto liver. Serve with a mixed leaf salad, if you like.

prep + cook time 40 minutes **serves** 4
nutritional count per serving 50.6g total fat (24.6g saturated fat); 3377kJ (808 cal); 46.9g carbohydrate; 46.6g protein; 2.8g fibre

Veal parmigiana

4 veal steaks (320g)
¼ cup (35g) plain (all-purpose) flour
1 egg
1 tablespoon water
⅓ cup (25g) stale breadcrumbs
30g (1 ounce) butter
⅓ cup (80ml) olive oil
1½ cups (150g) coarsely grated
mozzarella cheese
⅓ cup (25g) finely grated
parmesan cheese
tomato sauce
1 tablespoon olive oil
1 medium brown onion (150g),
chopped finely

1 stalk celery (150g), trimmed,
chopped finely
1 medium red capsicum (bell
pepper) (200g), chopped finely
1 clove garlic, crushed
410g (13 ounces) canned
crushed tomatoes
2 teaspoons white sugar
1 tablespoon tomato paste
1½ cups (375ml) chicken stock
1 tablespoon finely chopped
fresh flat-leaf parsley
1 tablespoon finely chopped
fresh basil

1 Make tomato sauce.
2 Pound veal out thinly between layers of plastic wrap. Coat veal in flour; shake off excess. Dip veal in combined beaten egg and the water; press breadcrumbs firmly onto veal. Refrigerate 10 minutes.
3 Preheat oven to 180°C/350°F.
4 Heat butter and half the oil in large frying pan; cook veal, in batches, until browned both sides. Remove from pan.
5 Place veal in large shallow ovenproof dish; top with mozzarella, drizzle with tomato sauce, sprinkle with parmesan. Drizzle over remaining oil.
6 Bake veal about 20 minutes or until browned lightly. Serve with a mixed leaf salad, if you like.
tomato sauce Heat oil in medium frying pan; cook onion, celery, capsicum and garlic, stirring, until onion is soft. Remove from heat. Push undrained tomatoes through a sieve into pan; discard solids. Add sugar, paste and stock. Cover; bring to the boil. Reduce heat; simmer, covered, 30 minutes. Uncover; simmer until sauce is thick. Stir in herbs.

prep + cook time 1 hour 10 minutes **serves** 4
nutritional count per serving 42g total fat (14.8g saturated fat); 2592kJ (620 cal); 21g carbohydrate; 37g protein; 3.7g fibre

Veal with artichokes, olives and lemon

1 medium unpeeled lemon (140g),
  chopped coarsely
4 medium globe artichokes (800g)
1.2kg (2½ pounds) diced veal neck
¼ cup (35g) plain (all-purpose)
  flour
60g (2 ounces) butter
¼ cup (60ml) olive oil
1 medium brown onion (150g),
  chopped finely
1 medium carrot (120g),
  chopped finely
2 cloves garlic, chopped finely

2 sprigs fresh marjoram
2 sprigs fresh oregano
1 cup (250ml) dry white wine
2 cups (500ml) chicken stock
1 cup (150g) seeded
  kalamata olives
2 teaspoons finely grated
  lemon rind
2 tablespoons lemon juice
2 tablespoons fresh
  oregano leaves
1 medium lemon (140g), extra,
  cut into six wedges

1 Place chopped lemon in large bowl half-filled with cold water.
Discard outer leaves from artichokes; cut tips from remaining leaves.
Trim then peel stalks. Quarter artichokes lengthways; using teaspoon,
remove and discard chokes. Place in lemon water.
2 Preheat oven to 160°C/325°F.
3 Coat veal in flour; shake off excess. Heat butter and 2 tablespoons
of the oil in large flameproof casserole dish; cook veal, in batches,
until browned all over. Remove from pan.
4 Heat remaining oil in same dish; cook onion, carrot, garlic, marjoram
and oregano sprigs, stirring, until vegetables soften. Add wine; bring
to the boil. Return veal to dish with stock, cover; cook in oven 1 hour.
5 Add artichokes; cook in oven 30 minutes. Uncover; cook about
30 minutes or until veal is tender. Stir in olives, rind and juice. Divide
among serving plates; top with oregano leaves. Serve with lemon wedges
and penne, if you like.

prep + cook time 3 hours **serves** 6
nutritional count per serving 21.6g total fat (7.4g saturated fat);
2040kJ (488 cal); 14.6g carbohydrate; 50.2g protein; 3.4g fibre

Osso buco

12 pieces veal osso buco (3.5kg)
¼ cup (35g) plain (all-purpose) flour
¼ cup (60ml) olive oil
45g (1½ ounces) butter
1 medium brown onion (150g), chopped coarsely
2 cloves garlic, crushed
3 stalks celery (450g), trimmed, chopped coarsely
2 large carrots (360g), chopped coarsely
4 medium tomatoes (600g), chopped coarsely
2 tablespoons tomato paste
1 cup (250ml) dry white wine
1 cup (250ml) beef stock
410g (13 ounces) canned crushed tomatoes
3 sprigs fresh thyme
¼ cup coarsely chopped fresh flat-leaf parsley
gremolata
1 tablespoon finely grated lemon rind
⅓ cup finely chopped fresh flat-leaf parsley
2 cloves garlic, chopped finely

1 Coat veal in flour, shake off excess. Heat oil in large flameproof dish; cook veal, in batches, until browned all over. Remove from dish.
2 Melt butter in same dish; cook onion, garlic, celery and carrot, stirring, until vegetables soften. Stir in remaining ingredients.
3 Return veal to dish, fitting pieces upright and tightly together in a single layer; bring to the boil. Reduce heat; simmer, covered, 1¾ hours. Uncover; cook further 30 minutes.
4 Remove veal from dish; cover to keep warm. Bring sauce to the boil; boil, uncovered, about 10 minutes or until sauce thickens slightly.
5 Meanwhile, make gremolata.
6 Divide veal among serving plates; top with sauce, sprinkle with gremolata. Serve with soft polenta or mashed potato, if you like.
gremolata Combine ingredients in small bowl.

prep + cook time 2 hours 45 minutes **serves** 4
nutritional count per serving 16.3g total fat (5.2g saturated fat); 2056kJ (492 cal); 14g carbohydrate; 63.2g protein; 6g fibre

Veal marsala

8 veal schnitzels (800g)
45g (1½ ounces) butter
2 shallots (50g), chopped finely
2 teaspoons plain (all-purpose) flour
½ cup (125ml) marsala
½ cup (125ml) beef stock

1 Melt half the butter in large frying pan; cook veal, in batches, until cooked as desired. Remove from pan; cover to keep warm.
2 Melt remaining butter in same pan; cook shallot, stirring, until soft. Add flour; cook, stirring, 2 minutes. Stir in marsala; bring to the boil. Reduce heat; simmer, uncovered, 2 minutes. Add stock; bring to the boil. Reduce heat; simmer, uncovered, about 4 minutes or until sauce has reduced by half.
3 Serve veal topped with sauce; serve with zucchini, if you like.

prep + cook time 25 minutes **serves** 4
nutritional count per serving 12.3g total fat (6.9g saturated fat); 1471kJ (351 cal); 5.6g carbohydrate; 45.5g protein; 0.2g fibre

Veal scaloppine

8 veal schnitzels (800g)
¼ cup (35g) plain (all-purpose) flour
2 tablespoons olive oil
20g (¾ ounce) butter
2 tablespoons lemon juice
¼ cup (60ml) dry white wine
1 clove garlic, crushed
¾ cup (180ml) chicken stock
2 tablespoons drained baby capers, rinsed
¼ cup coarsely chopped fresh flat-leaf parsley

1 Coat veal in flour; shake off excess. Heat oil and butter in large frying pan; cook veal, in batches. Remove from pan; cover to keep warm.
2 Add juice, wine and garlic to pan; bring to the boil. Reduce heat; simmer, uncovered, until liquid is reduced by half. Add stock; simmer, uncovered, 5 minutes. Remove from heat; stir in capers and parsley.
3 Serve veal topped with sauce, and accompany with mashed potato and roasted cherry truss tomatoes, if you like.

prep + cook time 30 minutes **serves** 4
nutritional count per serving 16.6g total fat (4.9g saturated fat); 1572kJ (376 cal); 7.7g carbohydrate; 46.3g protein; 0.8g fibre

Veal saltimbocca

8 veal schnitzels (800g)
8 slices prosciutto (120g)
16 fresh sage leaves
45g (1½ ounces) butter
1 cup (250ml) dry white wine
1 tablespoon lemon juice
2 tablespoons coarsely chopped fresh sage

1 Top each piece of veal with prosciutto and sage leaves. Fold in half to secure filling; secure with toothpicks or small skewers.
2 Melt half the butter in large frying pan; cook veal, in batches, until cooked as desired. Remove from pan; cover to keep warm.
3 Add wine to same pan; bring to the boil. Boil, uncovered, until reduced by half. Stir in remaining butter, juice and sage.
4 Remove toothpicks from veal, serve with sauce; accompany with steamed green beans and baby new potatoes, if you like.

prep + cook time 30 minutes **serves** 4
nutritional count per serving 13g total fat (6.8g saturated fat); 1509kJ (361 cal); 0.5g carbohydrate; 50.3g protein; 0g fibre

PORK

Pork fillet and pancetta kebabs

8 x 15cm (6-inch) stalks fresh rosemary
625g (1¼ pounds) pork fillet, cut into 2cm (¾-inch) pieces
8 slices pancetta (120g), halved
1 large red capsicum (bell pepper) (350g), cut into 24 pieces
⅓ cup (80ml) olive oil
1 clove garlic, crushed

1 Remove leaves from bottom two-thirds of each rosemary stalk; reserve 2 tablespoons leaves, chop finely. Sharpen trimmed ends of stalks to a point.
2 Wrap each piece of pork in one slice of pancetta; thread with capsicum, alternately, onto stalks. Brush kebabs with combined chopped rosemary, oil and garlic.
3 Cook kebabs on heated oiled grill plate (or grill or grill pan), brushing frequently with rosemary mixture, until cooked.

prep + cook time 30 minutes **serves** 4
nutritional count per serving 23.6g total fat (4.4g saturated fat); 1601kJ (383 cal); 3.1g carbohydrate; 39.5g protein; 1g fibre

Braised pork with pancetta and fennel

2 tablespoons olive oil
1.5kg (3 pounds) pork shoulder,
    rolled and tied
2 cloves garlic, crushed
1 medium brown onion (150g),
    chopped coarsely
½ small fennel bulb (100g),
    chopped coarsely
8 slices hot pancetta (120g),
    chopped coarsely
1 tablespoon tomato paste
½ cup (125ml) dry white wine
410g can whole tomatoes

1 cup (250ml) chicken stock
1 cup (250ml) water
2 sprigs fresh rosemary
2 large fennel bulbs (1kg),
    halved, sliced thickly
spice rub
1 teaspoon fennel seeds
2 teaspoons dried oregano
½ teaspoon cayenne pepper
1 tablespoon cracked
    black pepper
1 tablespoon sea salt
2 teaspoons olive oil

1 Preheat oven to 180°C/350°F.
2 Heat oil in large flameproof casserole dish; cook pork, uncovered,
until browned all over. Remove pork from dish; discard all but 1 tablespoon
of the oil in dish.
3 Cook garlic, onion, chopped fennel and pancetta in same dish,
stirring, until onion softens. Add paste; cook, stirring, 2 minutes.
4 Combine ingredients for spice rub in small bowl; rub all over pork.
5 Return pork to dish with wine, undrained tomatoes, stock, the water
and rosemary; bring to the boil. Cover; cook in oven 1 hour.
6 Add sliced fennel; cook, covered, in oven 1 hour. Remove pork from
dish; discard rind. Cover to keep warm.
7 Meanwhile, cook braising liquid in dish over medium heat, uncovered,
until thickened slightly. Return sliced pork to dish; serve pork and sauce
with warm italian bread, if you like.

prep + cook time 3 hours 15 minutes **serves** 6
nutritional count per serving 32.8g total fat (10.7g saturated fat);
2525kJ (604 cal); 7.5g carbohydrate; 66.5g protein; 4.6g fibre

Pork cutlets with fennel and apple relish

2 tablespoons cider vinegar
¼ cup (60ml) olive oil
1 tablespoon dijon mustard
2 teaspoons caster sugar
4 pork cutlets (1kg)
fennel and apple relish
1 large unpeeled green apple (200g), chopped finely
1 small red onion (100g), chopped finely
1 medium fennel bulb (300g), trimmed, chopped finely

1 Whisk vinegar, oil, mustard and sugar in medium bowl.
2 Combine pork and 2 tablespoons of the dressing in large bowl.
3 Make fennel and apple relish.
4 Meanwhile, cook drained pork on heated oiled grill plate (or grill or grill pan) until browned both sides and cooked as desired, brushing with marinade occasionally.
5 Serve pork with relish and crushed potato, if you like.
fennel and apple relish Combine ingredients in medium bowl with remaining dressing.

prep + cook time 35 minutes **serves** 4
nutritional count per serving 31.2g total fat (7.9g saturated fat);
1877kJ (449 cal); 9.6g carbohydrate; 32g protein; 2.3g fibre

Italian braised sausages with beans

8 thick pork sausages (1.2kg)
800g (28 ounces) canned diced tomatoes
⅓ cup (80ml) water
200g (6½ ounces) drained marinated antipasto vegetables
410g (13 ounces) canned cannellini beans, rinsed, drained
½ cup loosely packed fresh baby basil leaves

1 Cook sausages in heated oiled large saucepan until browned.
Remove from pan; cut in half lengthways.
2 Bring undrained tomatoes and the water to the boil in same pan.
Return sausages to pan with antipasto vegetables; simmer, covered,
15 minutes. Add beans; simmer, uncovered, about 10 minutes or
until thickened slightly. Remove pan from heat, stir in half the basil.
3 Serve sausages and beans topped with remaining basil.

prep + cook time 35 minutes **serves** 4
nutritional count per serving 68.5g total fat (27.3g saturated fat);
3708kJ (887 cal); 20.6g carbohydrate; 43.1g protein; 12.1g fibre
tip We used semi-dried tomatoes, marinated artichokes, grilled eggplant
and red capsicum for the antipasto mix; however, any combination of
vegetables can be used.

Bollito misto

2 tablespoons olive oil
4 thin italian pork sausages (320g)
500g (1 pound) beef chuck steak, cut into 2cm (¾-inch) pieces
500g (1 pound) chicken thigh fillets, cut into 2cm (¾-inch) pieces
1 medium brown onion (150g), chopped coarsely
1 clove garlic, crushed
2 cups (500ml) beef stock
1 cup (250ml) water
2 bay leaves
2 medium carrots (240g), chopped coarsely
2 medium potatoes (400g), chopped coarsely
¼ cup (50g) drained capers, rinsed, chopped coarsely
4 anchovy fillets, chopped finely
2 teaspoons finely grated lemon rind
1 tablespoon lemon juice
1 cup coarsely chopped fresh flat-leaf parsley

1 Heat half the oil in large saucepan; cook sausages until browned.
Remove from pan; chop coarsely.
2 Cook beef and chicken, in batches, in same pan, until browned.
Remove from pan.
3 Heat remaining oil in same pan; cook onion and garlic, stirring,
until onion softens. Return meats to pan with stock, the water and bay
leaves; bring to the boil. Reduce heat; simmer, covered, 1½ hours.
4 Add carrot and potato to pan; simmer, uncovered, about 30 minutes
or until vegetables soften. Add capers, anchovy, rind and juice; cook,
stirring, until hot. Remove from heat; stir in parsley.

prep + cook time 3 hours **serves** 4
nutritional count per serving 42.2g total fat (13.8g saturated fat);
3035kJ (726 cal); 20.5g carbohydrate; 64.1g protein; 5.7g fibre

Pork ragu with pappardelle

2 x 5cm (2-inch) thick pork scotch fillet (750g)
2 tablespoons plain (all-purpose) flour
1 tablespoon olive oil
20g (¾ ounce) butter
1 medium leek (350g), sliced
3 cloves garlic, sliced
1 medium fennel bulb (200g), sliced thinly, reserve fennel tops
½ cup (125ml) dry white wine
1½ cups (375ml) chicken stock
500g (1 pound) pappardelle pasta
2 teaspoons balsamic vinegar
½ cup (80g) seeded green olives

1 Preheat oven to 160°C/325°F.
2 Toss pork in flour; shake away excess. Heat oil and butter in flameproof casserole dish; add pork, cook until browned all over.
3 Add leek, garlic and fennel to dish; stir over medium heat until softened. Add wine; bring to the boil. Reduce heat; simmer, uncovered, until wine is almost evaporated. Add stock; bring to the boil.
4 Cover dish; cook in oven about 2 hours or until pork is tender, turning halfway. Cool pork 10 minutes, then tear into small pieces.
5 Meanwhile, cook pasta in large saucepan of boiling water until tender; drain. Return to pan.
6 Reheat pork and sauce, stir in vinegar and olives; add to pasta, toss gently to combine. Serve sprinkled with reserved fennel tops.

prep + cook time 2 hours 35 minutes **serves** 6
nutritional count per serving 12g total fat (4.2g saturated fat); 2274kJ (544 cal); 62.8g carbohydrate; 39.3g protein; 5.3g fibre

Sage roasted pork loin

10 fresh sage leaves
1kg (2 pounds) boneless loin of pork, rind off
2 tablespoons sea salt flakes
2 tablespoons crushed dried green peppercorns
2 tablespoons coarsely chopped fresh sage
1 tablespoon olive oil

1 Lay sage leaves in the middle of pork loin; roll pork to enclose leaves. Tie pork at 10cm (4-inch) intervals with kitchen string.
2 Combine salt, peppercorns and chopped sage in small bowl. Brush pork with oil; rub with salt mixture.
3 Place pork in disposable aluminium baking dish. Cook pork in preheated covered barbecue, using indirect heat, about 1 hour or until cooked through.
4 Cover pork loosely with foil; stand 10 minutes before slicing.

prep + cook time 1 hour 15 minutes **serves** 6
nutritional count per serving 5.7g total fat (1.3g saturated fat); 861kJ (206 cal); 0.7g carbohydrate; 37.7g protein; 0g fibre

LAMB

Tomato braised lamb shanks

2 tablespoons olive oil
16 french-trimmed lamb shanks (4kg)
1 large red onion (300g), sliced thinly
1 clove garlic, crushed
2 tablespoons tomato paste
1 cup (250ml) dry red wine
2 cups (500ml) chicken stock
1 cup (250ml) water
410g (13 ounces) canned diced tomatoes
2 tablespoons coarsely chopped fresh rosemary
creamy polenta
3 cups (750ml) water
2 cups (500ml) milk
1 cup (250ml) chicken stock
1½ cups (250g) polenta
½ cup (40g) coarsely grated parmesan cheese
1 cup (250ml) pouring cream

1 Preheat oven to 200°C/400°F.
2 Heat half the oil in large baking dish; brown shanks, in batches.
Remove from dish.
3 Heat remaining oil in same dish; cook onion and garlic, stirring,
until onion softens. Add paste; cook, stirring, 2 minutes. Add wine;
bring to the boil. Boil, uncovered, until liquid reduces by about half.
4 Return lamb to dish with stock, the water, undrained tomatoes and
rosemary; cover, cook in oven, turning lamb occasionally, about 3 hours.
Remove lamb from dish; cover to keep warm. Reserve pan juices.
5 Make creamy polenta.
6 Divide polenta among serving plates; top with lamb, drizzle with juices.
creamy polenta Bring the water, milk and stock to the boil in medium
saucepan. Gradually stir in polenta; cook, stirring, about 5 minutes or
until polenta thickens slightly. Stir in cheese and cream.

prep + cook time 4 hours **serves** 8
nutritional count per serving 28g total fat (14.8g saturated fat);
2826kJ (676 cal); 30.3g carbohydrate; 69.1g protein; 2.3g fibre

Braised lamb shanks with white bean puree

1 tablespoon olive oil
8 french-trimmed lamb shanks (2kg)
1 large red onion (300g),
    chopped coarsely
2 cloves garlic, crushed
1 cup (250ml) chicken stock
2 cups (500ml) water
410g (13 ounces) canned
    diced tomatoes
1 tablespoon fresh rosemary
4 drained anchovy fillets,
    chopped coarsely
2 large red capsicums
    (bell pepper) (700g)
2 large green capsicums
    (bell pepper) (700g)

white bean puree
20g (¾ ounce) butter
1 small brown onion (80g),
    chopped finely
1 clove garlic, crushed
¼ cup (60ml) dry white wine
¾ cup (180ml) chicken stock
2 x 410g (13 ounces) canned
    white beans, rinsed, drained
2 tablespoons pouring cream

1 Heat oil in large deep saucepan; cook lamb, in batches, until browned all over. Remove from pan.
2 Cook onion and garlic in same pan, stirring, until onion softens. Add stock, the water, undrained tomatoes, rosemary and anchovy; bring to the boil. Return lamb to pan, reduce heat; simmer, covered, 1 hour, stirring occasionally. Uncover; simmer about 45 minutes or until lamb is tender.
3 Meanwhile, quarter capsicums; discard seeds and membranes. Roast under hot grill or in very hot oven, skin-side up, until skin blisters and blackens. Cover capsicum pieces with plastic wrap or paper for 5 minutes; peel away skin, slice thickly.
4 Meanwhile, make white bean puree.
5 Add capsicum to lamb; cook 5 minutes. Serve lamb with bean puree.
white bean puree Melt butter in medium frying pan; cook onion and garlic, stirring, until onions softens. Add wine; cook, stirring, until liquid is reduced by half. Add stock and beans; bring to the boil. Reduce heat; simmer, uncovered, about 10 minutes or until liquid is almost evaporated. Blend or process bean mixture and cream until smooth.

prep + cook time 3 hours 10 minutes **serves** 4
nutritional count per serving 18.8g total fat (8.4g saturated fat); 2312kJ (553 cal); 21g carbohydrate; 72.1g protein; 8.6g fibre

Lamb, bocconcini and gremolata stacks

4 lamb leg steaks (600g)
1 tablespoon olive oil
1 large red capsicum (bell pepper) (350g)
2 tablespoons lemon juice
125g (4 ounces) bocconcini cheese, sliced thinly
gremolata
2 teaspoons finely grated lemon rind
2 cloves garlic, chopped finely
2 tablespoons finely chopped fresh basil

1 Preheat grill (broiler).
2 Make gremolata.
3 Using meat mallet, gently pound lamb between sheets of plastic
wrap until 1cm (½-inch) thick. Heat oil in large frying pan; cook lamb,
in batches, until cooked as desired. Place lamb on oven tray.
4 Meanwhile, quarter capsicum, discard seeds and membranes.
Roast under hot grill, skin-side up, until skin blisters and blackens.
Cover capsicum pieces in plastic or paper 5 minutes; peel away skin
then slice thickly. Combine capsicum and juice in small bowl.
5 Divide capsicum and bocconcini among lamb steaks; place under
grill about 5 minutes or until cheese melts.
6 Serve stacks sprinkled with gremolata.
gremolata Combine ingredients in small bowl.

prep + cook time 35 minutes **serves** 4
nutritional count per serving 16.7g total fat (6.8g saturated fat);
1346kJ (322 cal); 3.4g carbohydrate; 38.8g protein; 1.2g fibre

Lamb chops with roasted capsicum mayonnaise

125g (4 ounces) roasted red capsicum (bell pepper)
½ cup (150g) whole-egg mayonnaise
8 lamb mid-loin chops (800g)

1 Blend or process capsicum and mayonnaise until smooth.
2 Cook lamb, in batches, on heated oiled grill plate (or grill or grill pan) until browned both sides and cooked as desired.
3 Serve lamb topped with capsicum mayonnaise.

prep + cook time 25 minutes **serves** 4
nutritional count per serving 32.2g total fat (10.6g saturated fat); 1869kJ (447 cal); 8.2g carbohydrate; 31.5g protein; 0.5g fibre

Lamb with lemon, artichoke and thyme

30g (1 ounce) butter
2 tablespoons plain (all-purpose) flour
1 cup (250ml) chicken stock
1 tablespoon olive oil
625g (1¼ pounds) lamb backstraps
½ cup (125ml) dry white wine
2 teaspoons finely grated lemon rind
¼ cup (60ml) lemon juice
125g (4 ounces) drained artichoke hearts, quartered
2 teaspoons finely chopped fresh thyme
½ cup (125ml) pouring cream

1 Heat butter in small saucepan; add flour, cook, stirring, until mixture bubbles and thickens. Gradually add stock; stirring, until mixture boils and thickens.
2 Heat oil in large frying pan; cook lamb, in batches, until cooked as desired. Remove from pan.
3 Deglaze pan with wine, add stock mixture, rind, juice, artichoke, thyme and cream; bring to the boil. Reduce heat; simmer about 5 minutes or until sauce thickens slightly.
4 Serve sliced lamb with sauce, accompany with vegetables, if you like.

prep + cook time 30 minutes **serves** 4
nutritional count per serving 38.3g total fat (19.9g saturated fat); 2195kJ (525 cal); 6.4g carbohydrate; 33.9g protein; 0.3g fibre

Mini lamb roasts with capsicum and pesto

155g (5 ounces) roasted red capsicum (bell pepper) in oil
1 cup (70g) stale breadcrumbs
2 tablespoons (45g) basil pesto
45g (1½ ounces) rocket (arugula), chopped coarsely
¼ cup (20g) finely grated parmesan cheese
2 mini lamb roasts (700g)

1 Preheat oven to 200°C/400°F.

2 Drain oil from capsicum; reserve 2 tablespoons. Chop capsicum coarsely.

3 Heat reserved oil in medium frying pan; cook breadcrumbs, stirring, until browned lightly. Add pesto, rocket and capsicum; cook, stirring, until rocket wilts. Cool 5 minutes; stir in cheese.

4 Cut a horizontal slit in each roast to make a large pocket, but do not cut all the way through. Press half the bread mixture into each pocket; secure with toothpicks.

5 Heat oiled small baking dish over high heat; cook lamb, turning, until browned all over. Transfer to oven; roast, uncovered, about 20 minutes or until cooked through.

6 Remove toothpicks from lamb, serve with a mixed leaf salad, if you like.

prep + cook time 35 minutes **serves** 4
nutritional count per serving 32.9g total fat (10.4g saturated fat); 2165kJ (518 cal); 12.8g carbohydrate; 42.5g protein; 1.1g fibre

Italian-style lamb cutlets

8 french-trimmed lamb cutlets (400g)
125g (4 ounces) firm goat's cheese, crumbled
¼ cup finely chopped sun-dried tomatoes
2 tablespoons finely shredded fresh basil
4 slices prosciutto (60g), halved lengthways

1 Cut a small horizontal slit in the side of each lamb cutlets.
2 Combine cheese, tomatoes and basil in medium bowl. Press cheese mixture into lamb pockets. Wrap each cutlet with a slice of prosciutto.
3 Cook cutlets in heated oiled large frying pan until brown both sides and cooked through.

prep + cook time 30 minutes **serves** 4
nutritional count per serving 11.1g total fat (5.8g saturated fat);
790kJ (189 cal); 3.1g carbohydrate; 18.8g protein; 1.2g fibre

Honey-balsamic lamb and beetroot salad

750g (1½ pounds) lamb fillets
1 tablespoon honey
1 tablespoon balsamic vinegar
1 clove garlic, crushed
500g (1 pound) baby beetroot (beets)
2 teaspoons olive oil
1 lebanese cucumber (130g), seeded, diced
200g (6½ ounces) ricotta cheese, crumbled
honey balsamic dressing
¼ cup (60ml) olive oil
2 tablespoons balsamic vinegar
1 tablespoon honey
1 teaspoon dijon mustard

1 Combine lamb, honey, vinegar and garlic in medium bowl.
Cover; refrigerate 3 hours or overnight.
2 Preheat oven to 220°C/425°F.
3 Remove unblemished leaves from beetroot, reserve. Peel and
quarter beetroot. Place on oven tray; drizzle with oil. Roast about
30 minutes or until tender.
4 Meanwhile, cook lamb in heated oiled large frying pan until cooked
as desired. Cover lamb; stand 5 minutes then slice thinly.
5 Make honey balsamic dressing.
6 Place lamb, beetroot and beetroot leaves in large bowl with cucumber
and dressing; toss gently to combine. Sprinkle with cheese.
honey balsamic dressing Combine ingredients in small bowl.

prep + cook time 40 minutes (+ refrigeration) **serves** 4
nutritional count per serving 28.9g total fat (9.1g saturated fat);
2228kJ (533 cal); 19.2g carbohydrate; 47.9g protein; 2.8g fibre

VEGETARIAN

Wild mushroom risotto

15g (½ ounce) dried chanterelle mushrooms
15g (½ ounce) dried porcini mushrooms
1 litre (4 cups) chicken or vegetable stock
2 cups (500ml) water
50g (2 ounces) butter
125g (4 ounces) chestnut mushrooms, trimmed
125g (4 ounces) button mushrooms, sliced thickly
2 flat mushrooms (160g), halved, sliced thickly
4 shallots (100g), chopped finely
2 cloves garlic, crushed
2 cups (400g) arborio rice
½ cup (125ml) dry white wine
½ cup (40g) finely grated parmesan cheese
2 tablespoons finely chopped fresh chives

1 Bring chantarelle and porcini mushrooms, stock and the water to the boil in medium saucepan. Reduce heat; simmer, covered.
2 Meanwhile, melt 30g (1 ounce) of the butter in large saucepan, add remaining mushrooms; cook, stirring, until mushrooms are tender and liquid evaporates. Remove from pan.
3 Melt remaining butter in same pan; cook shallots and garlic, stirring, until shallots soften. Add rice; stir to coat rice in butter mixture. Return mushrooms cooked in butter to pan with wine; bring to the boil. Reduce heat; simmer, uncovered, until liquid has almost evaporated. Add 1 cup simmering mushroom stock mixture; cook, stirring, over low heat, until stock is absorbed. Continue adding stock mixture, in 1-cup batches, stirring, until absorbed between additions. Total cooking time should be about 25 minutes or until rice is tender. Stir in cheese and chives.

prep + cook time 40 minutes **serves** 4
nutritional count per serving 15.4g total fat (9.4g saturated fat); 2391kJ (572 cal); 82.2g carbohydrate; 17.9g protein; 4.4g fibre

Asparagus and goat's cheese risotto

3 cups (750ml) water
3 cups (750ml) vegetable stock
1 tablespoon olive oil
2 medium brown onions (300g), chopped finely
2 cloves garlic, crushed
2 cups (400g) arborio rice
½ cup (125ml) vermouth
185g (6 ounces) asparagus, chopped coarsely
½ cup (60g) frozen peas
¼ cup loosely packed fresh lemon thyme leaves
155g (5 ounces) soft goat's cheese, crumbled

1 Bring the water and stock to the boil in medium saucepan. Reduce heat; simmer, covered.
2 Heat oil in large saucepan; cook onion and garlic, stirring, until soft. Add rice; stir to coat in onion mixture. Add vermouth; cook, stirring, until liquid is almost evaporated. Stir in 1 cup of simmering stock mixture; cook, stirring, over low heat until stock is absorbed. Continue adding stock, in 1-cup batches, stirring, until stock is absorbed after each addition and rice is tender.
3 Add asparagus, peas, three-quarters of the thyme and half the cheese; cook, stirring, until asparagus is tender.
4 Serve risotto sprinkled with remaining thyme and cheese.

prep + cook time 40 minutes **serves** 4
nutritional count per serving 12g total fat (5g saturated fat); 2399kJ (574 cal); 89.9g carbohydrate; 16.9g protein; 3.6g fibre

Creamy polenta with slow-roasted mushrooms

155g (5 ounces) oyster mushrooms, halved
200g (6½ ounces) fresh shiitake mushrooms, halved
200g (6½ ounces) swiss brown mushrooms, halved
2 large flat mushrooms (350g), chopped coarsely
280g (9 ounces) vine-ripened tomatoes, chopped coarsely
1 small red onion (100g), sliced thinly
2 cloves garlic, sliced thinly
1 tablespoon olive oil
15g (½ ounce) dried porcini mushrooms
1 cup (250ml) boiling water
2 cups (500ml) milk
1 cup (250ml) cold water
¾ cup (125g) polenta
20g (¾ ounce) butter
⅓ cup (35g) finely grated parmesan cheese
1 cup firmly packed fresh flat-leaf parsley leaves
½ cup coarsely chopped fresh chives

1 Preheat oven to 160°C/325°F.
2 Combine oyster, shiitake, swiss brown and flat mushrooms in large baking dish with tomato, onion, garlic and oil. Roast about 30 minutes or until mushrooms are tender.
3 Meanwhile, soak porcini in the boiling water in small jug 15 minutes. Drain over small bowl; reserve liquid. Chop porcini finely.
4 Bring reserved porcini liquid, milk and the cold water to the boil in medium saucepan. Gradually add polenta, stirring. Reduce heat; cook, stirring, about 5 minutes or until polenta thickens slightly. Stir in porcini, butter and cheese.
5 Stir herbs into mushroom mixture. Divide polenta among serving plates; top with mushroom mixture.

prep + cook time 1 hour **serves** 4
nutritional count per serving 17.8g total fat (8.5g saturated fat); 1622kJ (388 cal); 39g carbohydrate; 18.6g protein; 9.1g fibre

Grilled herb polenta with semi-dried tomato and olive salad

2 cups (500ml) water
2 cups (500ml) vegetable stock
1 cup (170g) polenta
⅓ cup (25g) finely grated
parmesan cheese
1 tablespoon finely chopped
fresh flat-leaf parsley
1 tablespoon finely chopped
fresh basil

**semi-dried tomato
and olive salad**
125g (4 ounces) baby cos lettuce,
trimmed, leaves torn roughly
1⅓ cups (200g) drained
semi-dried tomatoes in oil
4 green onions (scallions),
sliced thinly
¼ cup (50g) sliced black olives
spiced mayonnaise
¾ cup (225g) mayonnaise
pinch cayenne pepper
¼ teaspoon ground cumin
¼ teaspoon ground coriander
¼ teaspoon ground turmeric
1 tablespoon lemon juice

1 Bring the water and stock to the boil in medium saucepan. Gradually add polenta, stirring constantly. Reduce heat; cook, stirring, 10 minutes or until polenta thickens. Stir in cheese, parsley and basil.
2 Spread polenta evenly into deep 19cm (7½-inch) square cake pan; cool 10 minutes. Cover; refrigerate about 3 hours or until firm.
3 Turn polenta onto board; trim edges. Cut into four squares, cut each square diagonally into two triangles. Cook polenta, in batches, on heated oiled grill plate (or grill or grill pan) until browned both sides.
4 Meanwhile, make tomato and olive salad. Make spiced mayonnaise.
5 Serve polenta topped with salad; drizzle with mayonnaise.
semi-dried tomato and olive salad Combine ingredients in medium bowl.
spiced mayonnaise Whisk ingredients in small bowl until combined.

prep + cook time 45 minutes (+ refrigeration) **serves** 4
nutritional count per serving 25.7g total fat (4.2g saturated fat);
2320kJ (555 cal); 62.4g carbohydrate; 13.8g protein; 9.6g fibre

Soft polenta with ratatouille

1 medium eggplant (300g), chopped coarsely
1 large red capsicum (bell pepper) (350g), chopped coarsely
410g (13 ounces) canned diced tomatoes
¼ cup loosely packed fresh baby basil leaves
cheesy polenta
1.25 litres (5 cups) water
1 cup (170g) polenta
1 cup (80g) finely grated parmesan cheese

1 Cook eggplant and capsicum in heated oiled large frying pan until tender. Add undrained tomatoes; simmer, uncovered, 5 minutes or until mixture thickens slightly.
2 Meanwhile, make cheesy polenta.
3 Serve polenta with ratatouille; sprinkle with basil.
cheesy polenta Bring the water to the boil in large saucepan; gradually stir in polenta. Reduce heat; cook, stirring, about 10 minutes or until polenta thickens. Remove from heat; stir in cheese. Stand 3 minutes before serving.

prep + cook time 30 minutes **serves** 4
nutritional count per serving 7.9g total fat (4.2g saturated fat); 1208kJ (289 cal); 37.5g carbohydrate; 14g protein; 5.3g fibre

Artichokes with lemon herb butter

75g (2½ ounces) butter, softened
2 teaspoons finely grated lemon rind
1 tablespoon finely chopped fresh flat-leaf parsley
2 teaspoons finely chopped fresh basil
4 medium globe artichokes (800g)

1 Combine butter, rind and herbs in small bowl. Place on piece of plastic wrap; shape into log, wrap tightly. Freeze until firm.
2 Meanwhile, remove and discard tough outer leaves from artichokes. Trim stems so that artichoke bases sit flat.
3 Cook artichokes in large saucepan of boiling water about 40 minutes or until tender; drain.
4 Serve hot artichokes topped with slices of herb butter, and lemon wedges, if you like.

prep + cook time 50 minutes (+ freezing) **serves** 4
nutritional count per serving 16.7g total fat (10.8g saturated fat); 723kJ (173 cal); 1.9g carbohydrate; 3.9g protein; 1.2g fibre

Eggplant parmigiana

2 large eggplants (1kg)
olive oil, for shallow-frying
½ cup (75g) plain (all-purpose) flour
4 eggs, beaten lightly
2 cups (200g) packaged breadcrumbs
3 cups (750ml) bottled tomato pasta sauce
1 cup (100g) coarsely grated mozzarella cheese
¼ cup (20g) finely grated parmesan cheese
⅓ cup loosely packed fresh oregano leaves

1 Using vegetable peeler, peel random strips of skin from eggplants; discard skins. Slice eggplants thinly.
2 Heat oil in large frying pan. Coat eggplant in flour; shake off excess. Dip in egg, then in breadcrumbs. Shallow-fry eggplant, in batches, until browned lightly. Drain on absorbent paper.
3 Preheat oven to 200°C/400°F. Oil 2.5-litre (10-cup) ovenproof dish.
4 Spread about one-third of the pasta sauce over base of dish. Top with about one-third of the eggplant, one-third of the cheeses and one-third of the oregano. Repeat layering.
5 Bake parmigiana, covered, 20 minutes. Uncover; bake about 10 minutes or until browned lightly.

prep + cook time 1 hour **serves** 6
nutritional count per serving 27.5g total fat (6.8g saturated fat); 2257kJ (540 cal); 49.4g carbohydrate; 19.9g protein; 8.3g fibre

Char-grilled radicchio parcels

3 cloves garlic, crushed
1 cup (150g) drained semi-dried tomatoes, chopped coarsely
410g (13 ounces) bocconcini cheese
1 cup coarsely chopped fresh basil
2 x 410g (13 ounces) cannned white beans, rinsed, drained
24 large radicchio leaves
1 tablespoon balsamic vinegar

1 Combine garlic, tomato, cheese, basil and beans in large bowl.
2 Plunge radicchio into large saucepan of boiling water then drain immediately; submerge in iced water to stop cooking process. When cool, drain; pat dry with absorbent paper.
3 Slightly overlap 2 leaves; place about ¼ cup of bean mixture in centre of leaves then roll, folding in edges to enclose filling. Repeat with remaining bean mixture and leaves.
4 Cook parcels, seam-side down, on heated oiled grill plate (or grill or grill pan) until filling is hot. Serve parcels drizzled with vinegar.

prep + cook time 25 minutes **serves** 4
nutritional count per serving 20g total fat (11g saturated fat); 1659kJ (397 cal); 18.9g carbohydrate; 28.7g protein; 13.8g fibre

Antipasto ciabatta rolls

1 medium eggplant (300g), sliced thinly
1 tablespoon ground cumin
4 ciabatta bread rolls
½ cup (130g) hummus
⅔ cup (100g) drained sun-dried tomatoes
45g (1 ½ ounces) baby rocket (arugula) leaves

1 Sprinkle eggplant with cumin.
2 Cook eggplant, in batches, on heated oiled grill plate (or grill or grill pan).
3 Split and toast cut sides of bread rolls; spread rolls with hummus, then sandwich eggplant, tomatoes and rocket among rolls.

prep + cook time 25 minutes **serves** 4
nutritional count per serving 8.3g total fat (1.4g saturated fat); 966kJ (231 cal); 25.9g carbohydrate; 8.9g protein; 8.4g fibre

Tomato, olive and ricotta tart

2 sheets puff pastry
¾ cup (105g) chopped semi-dried tomatoes
¾ cup (120g) seeded black olives
½ cup (120g) ricotta cheese, crumbled
½ small red onion (50g), sliced thinly
¼ cup fresh basil leaves, torn
1 egg, beaten lightly

1 Preheat oven to 200°C/400°F. Line oven tray with baking paper.
2 Cut a 16cm x 24cm (6½-inch x 9½-inch) rectangle from pastry; place on oven tray. Top with tomatoes, olives, cheese, onion and basil, leaving a 2cm (¾-inch) border on all sides; brush a little of the egg around edges.
3 Cut a 18cm x 24cm (7-inch x 9½-inch) rectangle from remaining pastry sheet; score pastry in a diamond pattern. Place scored pastry over filling, press edges to seal; brush pastry with egg.
4 Bake tart about 20 minutes or until golden brown.

prep + cook time 30 minutes **serves** 4
nutritional count per serving 25.1g total fat (12.5g saturated fat); 1965kJ (470 cal); 46.9g carbohydrate; 11.5g protein; 5.8g fibre

Kumara, rocket and pine nut frittata

1 large kumara (orange sweet potato) (500g), peeled, sliced thinly
45g (1 ½ ounces) baby rocket (arugula) leaves, trimmed
⅓ cup (50g) roasted pine nuts
¾ cup (60g) coarsely grated parmesan cheese
6 eggs
½ cup (125ml) pouring cream

1 Preheat oven to 200°C/400°F. Oil deep 20cm (8-inch) square cake pan; line base and sides with baking paper.
2 Boil, steam or microwave kumara until tender; drain. Cool.
3 Layer kumara, rocket, nuts and cheese in pan in two layers.
4 Whisk eggs and cream in medium bowl; pour into pan.
5 Bake frittata about 25 minutes or until set. Stand in pan 5 minutes before serving. Serve with a rocket salad, if you like.

prep + cook time 35 minutes **serves** 4
nutritional count per serving 33.2g total fat (13g saturated fat); 1952kJ (467 cal); 17g carbohydrate; 20.3g protein; 2.7g fibre

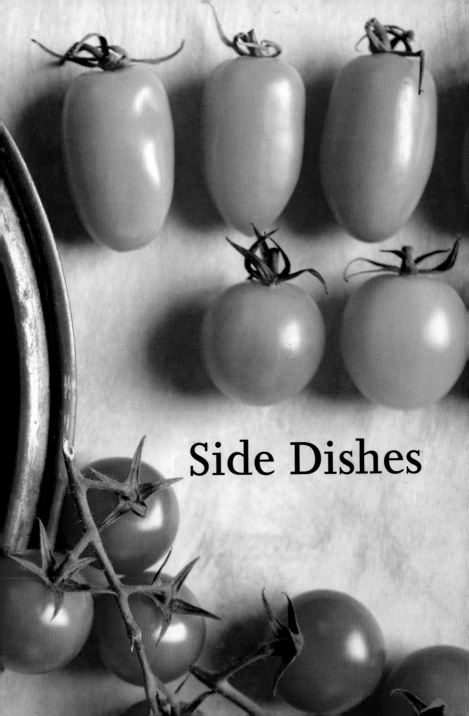

Side Dishes

Pumpkin, fennel and gorgonzola bake

800g (1¾ pounds) pumpkin, peeled, sliced thinly
2 baby fennel bulbs with fronds (260g)
125g (4 ounces) gorgonzola cheese, crumbled coarsely
1 tablespoon plain (all-purpose) flour
2 cups (500ml) pouring cream
½ cup (35g) stale breadcrumbs

1 Preheat oven to 200°C/400°F. Oil shallow 1-litre (4-cup) baking dish.
2 Boil, steam or microwave pumpkin until tender.
3 Slice fennel and fronds thinly. Layer fennel, half the fronds, three-quarters of the cheese and the pumpkin in dish.
4 Blend flour with a little of the cream in small saucepan; stir in remaining cream. Stir over heat until mixture boils and thickens; pour into dish. Cover dish with foil; bake 20 minutes.
5 Preheat grill (broiler).
6 Remove foil from dish; sprinkle with breadcrumbs and remaining cheese. Place under grill until browned. Serve sprinkled with remaining fennel fronds.

prep + cook time 35 minutes **serves** 4
nutritional count per serving 65.2g total fat (42.8g saturated fat); 3064kJ (733 cal); 22.9g carbohydrate; 14g protein; 3.5g fibre

Tiella

2 small eggplants (460g)
2 tablespoons coarse cooking salt
1kg (2 pounds) medium tomatoes, peeled, seeded, chopped finely
1 medium brown onion (150g), chopped finely
2 stalks celery (300g), trimmed, chopped finely
2 cloves garlic, crushed
1 tablespoon finely chopped fresh oregano
1 tablespoon finely chopped fresh flat-leaf parsley
1kg (2 pounds) sebago potatoes, peeled
¼ cup (60ml) olive oil
2 tablespoons fresh oregano leaves

1 Cut eggplants into thin slices, sprinkle with salt; stand in colander
in sink 30 minutes. Rinse eggplant well under cold water; pat dry with
absorbent paper.
2 Preheat oven to 180°C/350°F. Oil shallow 3-litre (12-cup) baking dish.
3 Combine tomato, onion, celery, garlic, chopped oregano and parsley
in medium bowl.
4 Using sharp knife, mandoline or V-slicer, cut potatoes into 2mm (⅛-inch)
slices; pat dry with absorbent paper. Place half the potato in dish; top with
half the eggplant, half the tomato mixture, then drizzle with half the oil.
Repeat layering with remaining potato, eggplant, tomato mixture and oil.
5 Cover dish with foil; bake 1 hour. Uncover; bake a further 30 minutes or
until vegetables are tender. Sprinkle tiella with oregano leaves.

prep + cook time 2 hours 10 minutes (+ standing) **serves** 8
nutritional count per serving 7.2g total fat (1g saturated fat);
723kJ (173 cal); 20.1g carbohydrate; 4.6g protein; 4.6g fibre

Creamy garlic mash

1kg (2 pounds) potatoes, chopped coarsely
3 cups (750ml) milk
1 clove garlic, peeled
45g (1½ ounces) butter, softened

1 Bring potato, milk and garlic to the boil in medium saucepan. Reduce heat; simmer, partially covered, about 15 minutes or until potato is soft.
2 Discard garlic. Strain potato over medium jug; reserve ⅔ cup of the milk.
3 Transfer potato to large bowl; mash with reserved milk and the butter until smooth.

prep + cook time 25 minutes **serves** 4
nutritional count per serving 15.8g total fat (10.2g saturated fat); 1542kJ (369 cal); 42g carbohydrate; 12.5g protein; 4.1g fibre

Braised baby leeks

16 baby pencil leeks (1.3kg)
30g (1 ounce) butter
⅔ cup (160ml) chicken stock
2 tablespoons dry white wine
1 teaspoon finely grated lemon rind
2 tablespoons lemon juice
¼ cup (20g) shaved parmesan cheese
¼ cup coarsely chopped fresh flat-leaf parsley

1 Carefully trim root end from leeks, leaving each leek in one piece.
Trim leeks into 15cm (6-inch) lengths; halve lengthways. Rinse under
cold water; drain.
2 Melt butter in large frying pan; cook leeks, 1 minute. Add stock,
wine, rind and juice; bring to the boil. Reduce heat; simmer, covered,
15 minutes or until leeks are tender. Uncover; simmer about 5 minutes or
until liquid has reduced by half.
3 Serve leeks drizzled with cooking liquid, topped with cheese and parsley.

prep + cook time 40 minutes **serves** 4
nutritional count per serving 8.7g total fat (5.2g saturated fat);
644kJ (154 cal); 8.3g carbohydrate; 6.5g protein; 6g fibre

Roasted balsamic onions

2 medium red onions (340g), quartered
2 medium brown onions (300g), quartered
2 bulbs garlic, halved horizontally
2 tablespoons olive oil
1 tablespoon balsamic vinegar
1 tablespoon light brown sugar

1 Preheat oven to 220°C/425°F.
2 Combine ingredients in medium baking dish.
3 Roast, brushing occasionally with pan juices, about 40 minutes or until onions and garlic are tender and caramelised.

prep + cook time 1 hour **serves** 4
nutritional count per serving 9.8g total fat (1.4g saturated fat); 702kJ (168 cal); 13.9g carbohydrate; 3.5g protein; 5.6g fibre

Prosciutto-wrapped bean bundles

200g (6½ ounces) yellow and green beans, trimmed
8 slices prosciutto (90g)
60g (2 ounces) butter
1 tablespoon drained baby capers, rinsed
1 tablespoon lemon juice
⅓ cup coarsely chopped fresh flat-leaf parsley

1 Cook beans in medium saucepan of boiling water until just tender.
Rinse under cold water; drain. Divide beans into eight equal bundles.
2 Place one slice of prosciutto on board; top with one bundle of beans.
Wrap prosciutto over beans; continue rolling to enclose beans tightly.
Repeat with remaining prosciutto and beans.
3 Cook bean bundles in heated oiled large frying pan until prosciutto
is crisp. Remove from pan; cover to keep warm.
4 Melt butter in same pan; cook capers, stirring, 1 minute. Stir in juice.
5 Serve bean bundles drizzled with caper mixture; sprinkle with parsley.

prep + cook time 30 minutes **serves** 8
nutritional count per serving 6.9g total fat (4.3g saturated fat);
347kJ (83 cal); 1.5g carbohydrate; 3.3g protein; 1.5g fibre

Crispy polenta, capsicum and walnut salad

1 litre (4 cups) water
1 cup (170g) polenta
½ cup (40g) coarsely grated parmesan cheese
½ cup (60g) coarsely grated cheddar cheese
1 tablespoon olive oil
75g (2½ ounces) baby spinach leaves
1 large red capsicum (bell pepper) (350g), sliced thinly
1 small red onion (100g), sliced thinly
walnut dressing
¼ cup (60ml) walnut oil
2 tablespoons white wine vinegar
1 clove garlic, crushed
⅓ cup (35g) coarsely chopped roasted walnuts
¼ cup coarsely chopped fresh flat-leaf parsley

1 Oil 19cm x 29cm (7½-inch x 11½-inch) slice pan.
2 Bring the water to the boil in medium saucepan. Gradually stir in polenta; reduce heat. Simmer, stirring, about 10 minutes or until polenta thickens. Stir in cheeses; spread polenta into pan. Refrigerate 1 hour or until firm.
3 Turn polenta onto board; cut into quarters then cut into 1cm (½-inch) cubes. Heat oil in large frying pan; cook polenta until browned lightly.
4 Meanwhile, make walnut dressing.
5 Place polenta in large bowl with dressing and remaining ingredients; toss gently to combine.
walnut dressing Place ingredients in screw-top jar; shake well.

prep + cook time 25 minutes (+ refrigeration) **serves** 4
nutritional count per serving 25g total fat (7.1g saturated fat); 1831kJ (438 cal); 35g carbohydrate; 16.4g protein; 4.6g fibre

Mixed leaf salad with cranberry dressing

1 baby cos lettuce (180g), trimmed, leaves separated
250g (8 ounces) rocket (arugula), trimmed
1 small radicchio (150g), trimmed, leaves separated
½ cup (40g) flaked almonds, roasted
½ cup (65g) dried cranberries
cranberry dressing
¼ cup (60m) olive oil
¼ cup (60ml) red wine vinegar
2 tablespoons cranberry juice
2 teaspoons dijon mustard
1 clove garlic, crushed
2 tablespoons cranberry sauce
½ small red onion (50g), chopped finely

1 Make cranberry dressing.
2 Combine lettuce, rocket and radicchio in large serving bowl; sprinkle with nuts and cranberries, drizzle with dressing.
cranberry dressing Blend oil, vinegar, juice, mustard, garlic and sauce until combined; stir in onion.

prep time 15 minutes **serves** 8
nutritional count per serving 10.1g total fat (1.2g saturated fat); 619kJ (148 cal); 10.7g carbohydrate; 2.8g protein; 2.4g fibre

Bean salad with creamy basil dressing

410g (13 ounces) canned butter beans, rinsed, drained
410g (13 ounces) canned borlotti beans, rinsed, drained
250g (8 ounces) cherry tomatoes, quartered
12 cherry bocconcini cheese (180g), halved
60g (2 ounces) baby rocket (arugula) leaves
½ cup (80g) roasted pine nuts
creamy basil dressing
2 tablespoons olive oil
2 tablespoons white wine vinegar
2 teaspoons white balsamic vinegar
2 tablespoons coarsely chopped fresh basil
¼ cup (60ml) pouring cream

1 Make creamy basil dressing.
2 Place salad ingredients in large bowl with dressing; toss gently to combine.
creamy basil dressing Combine oil, vinegars and basil in small bowl; whisk in cream until combined.

prep time 15 minutes **serves** 4
nutritional count per serving 37.1g total fat (11g saturated fat); 1944kJ (465 cal); 13g carbohydrate; 17.1g protein; 7.7g fibre

Mixed tomato caprese salad

4 small green tomatoes (360g), sliced thinly
4 small black tomatoes (360g), sliced thinly
4 small vine-ripened tomatoes (360g), sliced thinly
4 bocconcini cheese (240g), sliced thinly
⅓ cup coarsely chopped fresh basil
2 tablespoons olive oil
1 tablespoon balsamic vinegar

1 Layer tomato, cheese and basil on serving plate; drizzle with combined oil and vinegar.

prep time 20 minutes **serves** 4
nutritional count per serving 18.5g total fat (7.3g saturated fat);
1020kJ (244 cal); 5.2g carbohydrate; 13.1g protein; 3.3g fibre

Panzanella

1 litre (4 cups) water
250g (8 ounces) stale sourdough bread, cut into 2cm (¾-inch) slices
2 large tomatoes (440g), chopped coarsely
1 small red onion (100g), sliced thinly
2 lebanese cucumbers (260g), chopped coarsely
1 cup firmly packed fresh basil leaves
dressing
2 tablespoons olive oil
2 tablespoons red wine vinegar
1 clove garlic, crushed

1 Place the water in large shallow bowl; briefly dip bread slices into water. Pat dry with absorbent paper; tear bread into large chunks.
2 Make dressing.
3 Place bread in large bowl with dressing and remaining ingredients; toss gently to combine.
dressing Place ingredients in screw-top jar; shake well.

prep + cook time 20 minutes **serves** 4
nutritional count per serving 11g total fat (1.5g saturated fat); 1104kJ (264 cal); 33.2g carbohydrate; 7.5g protein; 6g fibre

Radicchio, pumpkin and haloumi salad

1kg (2 pounds) piece pumpkin, cut into 12 wedges
185g (6 ounces) haloumi cheese
1 medium radicchio (200g), trimmed, leaves separated
½ cup firmly packed fresh flat-leaf parsley leaves
¼ cup (50g) roasted pepitas
caper dressing
¼ cup (60ml) lemon juice
2 tablespoons olive oil
1 tablespoon drained baby capers, rinsed

1 Boil, steam or microwave pumpkin until tender; drain.
2 Cut cheese horizontally into four slices, cut each slice into four triangles.
3 Cook pumpkin and cheese, in batches, on heated oiled grill plate
(or grill or grill pan) until browned.
4 Meanwhile, make caper dressing.
5 Place radicchio in large bowl with dressing and parsley; toss gently
to combine. Divide salad among serving plates; top with pumpkin,
cheese and pepitas.
caper dressing Place ingredients in screw-top jar; shake well.

prep + cook time 30 minutes **serves** 4
nutritional count per serving 22g total fat (6.8g saturated fat);
1363kJ (326 cal); 15.2g carbohydrate; 14.8g protein; 5.2g fibre

Creamy polenta

3 cups (750ml) milk
1½ cups (125ml) water
1 cup (170g) polenta
½ cup (40g) finely grated parmesan cheese
30g (1 ounce) butter, chopped

1 Bring milk and the water to the boil in large saucepan.
2 Gradually add polenta to liquid, stirring constantly. Reduce heat; simmer, stirring, about 10 minutes or until polenta thickens. Stir in cheese and butter.

prep + cook time 20 minutes **serves** 4
nutritional count per serving 17.6g total fat (11.1g saturated fat); 1053kJ (252 cal); 9.4g carbohydrate; 13.7g protein; 1.2g fibre

Cheesy pesto polenta

2⅓ cups (580ml) milk
2⅓ cups (580ml) water
1 cup (170g) polenta
½ cup (40g) finely grated parmesan cheese
30g (1 ounce) butter, chopped
pesto
2 tablespoons finely grated parmesan cheese
2 tablespoons roasted pine nuts
2 tablespoons olive oil
1 clove garlic, crushed
1 cup firmly packed fresh basil leaves

1 Bring milk and the water to the boil in large saucepan.
2 Gradually add polenta to liquid, stirring constantly. Reduce heat; simmer, stirring, about 20 minutes or until polenta thickens.
3 Meanwhile, make pesto.
4 Stir pesto, cheese and butter into polenta.
pesto Blend or process ingredients until mixture forms a paste.

prep + cook time 35 minutes **serves** 4
nutritional count per serving 31.3g total fat (12.3g saturated fat); 2061kJ (493 cal); 37.1g carbohydrate; 14.9g protein; 2.6g fibre

Pizza

Napoletana pizza

280g (9 ounces) mozzarella cheese, sliced thinly
¼ cup coarsely torn fresh basil
pizza dough
2 teaspoons (7g) instant yeast
½ teaspoon salt
2½ cups (375g) plain (all-purpose) flour
1 cup (250ml) warm water
1 tablespoon olive oil
tomato pizza sauce
1 tablespoon olive oil
1 small white onion (80g), chopped finely
2 cloves garlic, crushed
410g (13 ounces) canned diced tomatoes
¼ cup (70g) tomato paste
1 teaspoon white sugar
1 tablespoon fresh oregano leaves

1 Make pizza dough. Make tomato pizza sauce.
2 Preheat oven to 200°C/400°F. Oil two pizza trays.
3 Divide pizza dough in half; roll each half on floured surface to form 30cm (12-inch) round. Place rounds on trays; spread each with half the tomato pizza sauce then top with cheese.
4 Bake pizzas about 15 minutes or until crust is golden and cheese is bubbling. Just before serving, sprinkle with basil.
pizza dough Combine yeast, salt and sifted flour in large bowl; gradually stir in combined water and oil. Knead dough on floured surface about 10 minutes or until smooth and elastic. Place dough in large oiled bowl; cover, stand in warm place about 30 minutes or until dough doubles in size. Punch down dough with fist; knead dough on floured surface until smooth. Roll out dough as required.
tomato pizza sauce Heat oil in medium frying pan; cook onion, stirring over low heat, until soft. Stir in garlic and undrained tomatoes, paste, sugar and oregano. Simmer, uncovered, 15 minutes or until mixture thickens.

prep + cook time 1 hour (+ standing) **serves** 6
nutritional count per serving 17.4g total fat (7.6g saturated fat); 1873kJ (448 cal); 50g carbohydrate; 20.5g protein; 4.3g fibre

Onion, anchovy and olive pizzetta

1 quantity pizza dough (see recipe page 322)
1 tablespoon olive oil
3 medium brown onions (450g), sliced thinly
2 tablespoons dry sherry
2 tablespoons tomato paste
12 drained anchovy fillets, chopped coarsely
¼ cup (40g) thinly sliced seeded kalamata olives
2 tablespoons fresh oregano leaves

1 Make pizza dough.
2 Heat oil in large frying pan; cook onion, stirring, until browned lightly.
Add sherry; cook, stirring, until sherry evaporates.
3 Preheat barbecue or grill plate to medium heat.
4 Divide dough into four portions; roll each portion to form 15cm (6-inch)
round pizzetta base. Cover barbecue grill plate with double thickness of
oiled foil. Place pizzetta bases on foil; cook, uncovered, 5 minutes.
5 Using metal tongs, turn bases; spread cooked sides with tomato paste.
Divide onion mixture among pizzetta; top with anchovies, olives and
oregano. Cook, covered, over low heat about 5 minutes or until bases
are cooked through.

prep + cook time 1 hour 10 minutes (+ standing) **serves** 6
nutritional count per serving 6.7g total fat (1g saturated fat);
1258kJ (301 cal); 46g carbohydrate; 10.1g protein; 4.1g fibre

Fig, prosciutto and goat's cheese pizzetta

1 quantity pizza dough (see recipe page 322)
⅓ cup (85g) bottled tomato pasta sauce
125g (4 ounces) goat's cheese, crumbled
2 large figs (160g), cut into thin wedges
4 slices prosciutto (60g), chopped coarsely
30g (1 ounce) baby rocket (arugula) leaves

1 Make pizza dough.
2 Preheat barbecue or grill plate to medium heat.
3 Divide dough into four portions; roll each portion to form 15cm (6-inch) round pizzetta base. Cover barbecue grill plate with double thickness of oiled foil. Place pizzetta bases on foil; cook, uncovered, 5 minutes.
4 Using metal tongs, turn bases; spread cooked side with pasta sauce. Divide cheese, fig and prosciutto among bases. Cook, covered, over low heat about 5 minutes or until bases are cooked through. Just before serving, top with rocket.

prep + cook time 1 hour (+ standing) **serves** 6
nutritional count per serving 7.9g total fat (2.9g saturated fat); 1363kJ (326 cal); 48.9g carbohydrate; 12.4g protein; 3.6g fibre

Pizza caprese

2 large pizza bases (770g)
½ cup (140g) tomato paste
4 large egg (plum) tomatoes (360g), sliced thinly
200g (6½ ounces) bocconcini cheese, halved
¼ cup finely shredded fresh basil

1 Preheat oven to 220°C/425°F. Oil two oven trays.
2 Spread bases with tomato paste; top with fresh tomato and cheese.
3 Bake pizzas about 15 minutes. Just before serving, top with basil.

prep + cook time 25 minutes **serves** 4
nutritional count per serving 14.6g total fat (6.1g saturated fat);
2658kJ (636 cal); 94.5g carbohydrate; 26.1g protein; 9g fibre
tip We used large (25cm/10-inch diameter) packaged pizza bases
for this recipe.

Smoked cheese and sopressa pizza

2 large pizza bases (770g)
½ cup (140g) tomato paste
90g (3 ounces) hot sopressa, sliced thinly
1 cup (150g) semi-dried tomatoes, drained, chopped coarsely
90g (3 ounces) smoked cheese, flaked
45g (1½ ounces) baby rocket (arugula) leaves

1 Preheat oven to 220°C/425°F. Oil two oven trays.
2 Spread bases with tomato paste; top with sopressa and tomato.
3 Bake pizzas about 15 minutes. Just before serving, top with cheese
and rocket.

prep + cook time 25 minutes **serves** 4
nutritional count per serving 24.6g total fat (5.4g saturated fat);
3352kJ (802 cal); 106.3g carbohydrate; 31.5g protein; 13.3g fibre
tip We used large (25cm/10-inch diameter) packaged pizza bases
for this recipe.

Pepperoni pizza

2 large pizza bases (770g)
½ cup (140g) tomato paste
125g (4 ounces) pepperoni, sliced thinly
4 slices (170g) roasted red capsicum (bell pepper), sliced thickly
¼ cup (40g) seeded kalamata olives
1 cup (80g) shaved parmesan cheese
2 tablespoons fresh oregano leaves

1 Preheat oven to 220°C/425°F. Oil two oven trays.
2 Spread bases with tomato paste; top with pepperoni, capsicum and olives, then sprinkle with cheese.
3 Bake pizzas about 15 minutes. Just before serving, top with oregano.

prep + cook time 25 minutes **serves** 4
nutritional count per serving 24.4g total fat (9g saturated fat); 3156kJ (755 cal); 97g carbohydrate; 31.9g protein; 8.3g fibre
tip We used large (25cm/10-inch diameter) packaged pizza bases for this recipe.

Chicken, artichoke and fetta pizza

2 large pizza bases (770g)
2 tablespoons olive oil
1 clove garlic, crushed
2 cups (320g) shredded cooked chicken
345g (11 ounces) marinated artichoke hearts in oil,
    drained, chopped coarsely
185g (6 ounces) fetta cheese, crumbled
⅓ cup finely shredded fresh mint
2 teaspoons finely grated lemon rind

1 Preheat oven to 220°C/425°F. Oil two oven trays.
2 Spread bases with combined oil and garlic; top with chicken,
artichoke and cheese.
3 Bake pizzas about 15 minutes. Just before serving, sprinkle with
mint and rind.

prep + cook time 25 minutes **serves** 4
nutritional count per serving 32.3g total fat (10.8g saturated fat);
3532kJ (845 cal); 89.9g carbohydrate; 44g protein; 8.3g fibre
tips We used large (25cm/10-inch diameter) packaged pizza bases
for this recipe.
You will need to purchase half a large barbecued chicken weighing about
450g to get the amount of shredded meat required for this recipe.

Ham, sage and fontina pizza

2 large pizza bases (770g)
1 tablespoon olive oil
2 cloves garlic, crushed
2 tablespoons finely chopped fresh sage
90g (3 ounces) thinly sliced ham
200g (6½ ounces) fontina cheese, sliced thinly

1 Preheat oven to 220°C/425°F. Oil two oven trays.
2 Spread bases with combined oil, garlic and sage; top with ham and cheese.
3 Bake pizzas about 10 minutes.

prep + cook time 20 minutes **serves** 4
nutritional count per serving 26.8g total fat (11.3g saturated fat); 3110kJ (744 cal); 89g carbohydrate; 33g protein; 6.5g fibre
tip We used large (25cm/10-inch diameter) packaged pizza bases for this recipe.

Prawn and grilled capsicum pizza

750g (1½ pounds) uncooked medium king prawns (shrimp)
1 tablespoon olive oil
4 cloves garlic, crushed
2 fresh small red thai chillies, chopped finely
4 small pizza bases (448g)
⅓ cup (90g) tomato paste
½ cup (50g) coarsely grated mozzarella cheese
280g (9 ounces) char-grilled red capsicum (bell pepper) in oil,
    drained, chopped coarsely
¼ cup (20g) shaved parmesan cheese
⅓ cup loosely packed fresh basil leaves

1 Preheat oven to 220°C/425°F. Oil two oven trays.
2 Shell and devein prawns. Place prawns in large bowl with oil, garlic
and chilli; toss gently to combine.
3 Cook prawn mixture in heated large frying pan until prawns are
changed in colour.
4 Spread bases with tomato paste; top with mozzarella, prawn mixture
and capsicum.
5 Bake pizzas about 15 minutes. Just before serving, sprinkle with
parmesan and basil.

prep + cook time 30 minutes **serves** 4
nutritional count per serving 16.9g total fat (4.4g saturated fat);
2328kJ (557 cal); 62.6g carbohydrate; 35.1g protein; 5.7g fibre
tip We used small (15cm/6-inch diameter) packaged pizza bases
for this recipe.

Kumara, fennel and caramelised onion pizza

1 large kumara (orange sweet potato) (500g), chopped coarsely
2 cloves garlic, crushed
1 tablespoon finely chopped fresh rosemary
1 teaspoon chilli flakes
2 tablespoons olive oil
45g (1½ ounces) butter
1 large red onion (300g), sliced thinly
4 large pitta breads (320g)
1 cup (260g) bottled tomato pasta sauce
2 cups (200g) coarsely grated mozzarella cheese
½ cup loosely packed fresh mint leaves

1 Preheat oven to 220°C/425°F.
2 Combine kumara, garlic, rosemary, chilli and oil in medium shallow baking dish. Roast about 20 minutes or until kumara is tender.
3 Meanwhile, melt butter in medium frying pan; cook onion, stirring occasionally, about 15 minutes or until caramelised.
4 Place pitta on oven trays; spread with pasta sauce. Divide kumara and onion among pitta; sprinkle with cheese.
5 Bake pizzas about 10 minutes or until pitta bases are crisp and topping is heated through. Just before serving, sprinkle with mint.

prep + cook time 45 minutes **serves** 4
nutritional count per serving 31g total fat (14.1g saturated fat); 2780kJ (665 cal); 68.8g carbohydrate; 25g protein; 7.3g fibre

Fennel and ricotta pizza

45g (1½ ounces) butter
2 medium fennel bulbs (600g), sliced thinly
½ teaspoon brown mustard seeds
1 teaspoon finely grated lemon rind
1 tablespoon lemon juice
1 teaspoon thinly sliced orange rind
1 tablespoon orange juice
4 large pitta breads (320g)
1 cup (260g) bottled tomato pasta sauce
1 cup (240g) ricotta cheese

1 Preheat oven to 220°C/425°F.
2 Melt butter in large frying pan; cook fennel, stirring occasionally, until tender. Stir in seeds, rinds and juices.
3 Place pitta on oven trays; spread with pasta sauce. Divide fennel mixture among pitta; sprinkle with cheese.
4 Bake pizzas about 10 minutes or until pitta bases are crisp and topping is heated through. Just before serving, sprinkle with fennel fronds, if you like.

prep + cook time 40 minutes **serves** 4
nutritional count per serving 17.4g total fat (10g saturated fat); 1827kJ (437 cal); 51.8g carbohydrate; 15.6g protein; 5.9g fibre

Potato and rosemary pizza

1 cup (250ml) warm water
1 teaspoon caster sugar
2 teaspoons (7g) instant yeast
2½ cups (375g) plain (all-purpose) flour
1 teaspoon coarse cooking salt
2 tablespoons olive oil
410g (13 ounces) baby new potatoes, sliced thinly
1 clove garlic, crushed
1 tablespoon coarsely chopped fresh rosemary

1 Combine the water, sugar and yeast in small jug. Stand in warm place about 10 minutes or until frothy.
2 Sift flour and salt into large bowl, add yeast mixture; mix to a soft dough. Knead dough on floured surface about 10 minutes or until smooth and elastic. Place dough in oiled large bowl. Cover; stand in warm place about 1 hour or until doubled in size.
3 Preheat oven to 220°C/425°F. Oil two oven trays.
4 Divide dough in half. Roll each portion into 18cm x 30cm (7-inch x 12-inch) rectangles; place on trays. Brush pizza bases with half the oil.
5 Combine potatoes, garlic, rosemary and remaining oil in medium bowl; layer potato mixture evenly over bases.
6 Bake pizzas about 30 minutes or until browned.

prep + cook time 45 minutes (+ standing) **serves** 6
nutritional count per serving 7g total fat (1g saturated fat);
1367kJ (327 cal); 54.5g carbohydrate; 8.9g protein; 4.1g fibre

Garlic pizza slices

1 cup (250ml) warm water
1 teaspoon caster sugar
2 teaspoons (7g) instant yeast
2½ cups (375g) plain (all-purpose) flour
1 teaspoon salt
1 tablespoon olive oil
2 cloves garlic, crushed
2 tablespoons finely grated parmesan cheese

1 Combine the water, sugar and yeast in small jug. Stand in warm place about 10 minutes or until frothy.
2 Sift flour and salt into large bowl, add yeast mixture; mix to a soft dough. Knead dough on floured surface about 10 minutes or until smooth and elastic. Place dough in oiled large bowl. Cover; stand in warm place about 1 hour or until dough is doubled in size.
3 Preheat oven to 220°C/425°F. Oil two oven trays.
4 Divide dough in half. Roll each portion into a 30cm (12-inch) round; place on trays. Brush bases with combined oil and garlic; sprinkle with cheese.
5 Bake pizzas about 20 minutes or until browned and crisp. Cut each pizza into 16 slices.

prep + cook time 1 hour (+ standing) **makes** 32 slices
nutritional count per slice 0.9g total fat (0.2g saturated fat);
209kJ (50 cal); 8.6g carbohydrate; 1.5g protein; 0.5g fibre

Sicilian stuffed pizza

¾ cup (180ml) warm water
2 teaspoons (7g) instant yeast
½ teaspoon sugar
2 cups (300g) plain (all-purpose)
   flour
1 teaspoon salt
⅓ cup (80ml) olive oil
1 cup (70g) stale breadcrumbs
2 cloves garlic, crushed
1 teaspoon ground fennel
1 small red onion (100g), chopped

250g (8 ounces) minced
   (ground) beef
125g (4 ounces) Italian salami,
   chopped finely
410g (13 ounces) canned
   crushed tomatoes
¼ cup (40g) roasted pine nuts
¼ cup coarsely chopped fresh
   flat-leaf parsley
½ cup (50g) finely grated
   fontina cheese

1 Combine the water, yeast and sugar in small bowl. Cover; stand in warm place about 15 minutes or until frothy. Sift flour and salt into large bowl, add yeast mixture and half of the oil; mix to a soft dough. Turn dough onto floured surface, knead about 5 minutes or until smooth and elastic. Place dough in large oiled bowl. Cover; stand in warm place about 1 hour or until dough is doubled in size.

2 Meanwhile, heat remaining oil in large frying pan; cook breadcrumbs and half the garlic, stirring, until crumbs are browned. Remove from pan.

3 Heat same pan; cook fennel, onion and remaining garlic, stirring, until onion just softens. Add mince; cook, stirring, until mince changes colour. Stir in salami and undrained tomatoes; bring to the boil. Reduce heat; simmer, uncovered, stirring occasionally, about 15 minutes or until liquid reduces by half. Remove from heat; stir in nuts and parsley. Cool.

4 Preheat oven to 220°C/425°F. Grease oven tray.

5 Knead dough on floured surface until smooth; divide dough in half. Roll each half into 30cm (12-inch) round. Place one round on tray; spread with breadcrumb mixture, mince mixture and cheese leaving a 1cm (½-inch) border. Top with remaining round; pinch edges to seal.

6 Bake pizza about 15 minutes or until browned lightly. Stand pizza on tray 10 minutes before cutting into slices. Serve pizza with a rocket and parmesan salad, if you like.

prep + cook time 1 hour 10 minutes (+ standing) **serves** 4
nutritional count per serving 49.1g total fat (12.1g saturated fat); 3720kJ (890 cal); 72.4g carbohydrate; 36.6g protein; 6.5g fibre

Dessert

Tiramisu

2 tablespoons ground espresso coffee
1 cup (250ml) boiling water
½ cup (125ml) marsala
250g (8-ounce) packet sponge finger biscuits
1¼ cups (310ml) thickened (heavy) cream
¼ cup (40g) icing (confectioner's) sugar
2 cups (500g) mascarpone cheese
2 tablespoons marsala, extra
2 teaspoons cocoa powder

1 Place coffee and the water in coffee plunger; stand 2 minutes before plunging. Combine coffee mixture and marsala in medium heatproof bowl; cool 10 minutes.
2 Place half the biscuits, in single layer, over base of deep 2-litre (8-cup) serving dish; drizzle with half the coffee mixture.
3 Beat cream and sifted icing sugar in small bowl with electric mixer until soft peaks form; transfer to large bowl. Fold in combined mascarpone and extra marsala.
4 Spread half the cream mixture over biscuits in dish. Dip remaining biscuits, one at a time, in coffee mixture; place over cream layer. Spread biscuits with remaining cream mixture.
5 Cover tiramisu; refrigerate 3 hours or overnight. Serve dusted with sifted cocoa.

prep + cook time 30 minutes (+ refrigeration) **serves** 8
nutritional count per serving 45g total fat (29.9g saturated fat);
2391kJ (572 cal); 25.8g carbohydrate; 6.5g protein; 0.5g fibre
tip You can use a 300ml carton of cream without affecting the recipe.

Hazelnut tiramisu

1 tablespoon instant coffee granules
2 tablespoons caster (superfine) sugar
⅔ cup (160ml) boiling water
⅓ cup (80ml) hazelnut-flavoured liqueur
½ cup (125ml) pouring cream
1 cup (250g) mascarpone cheese
12 sponge finger biscuits (140g)
¼ cup (25g) coarsely grated dark chocolate
½ cup (70g) coarsely chopped roasted hazelnuts

1 Dissolve coffee and half the sugar in the water in medium heatproof bowl; stir in liqueur. Cool.
2 Meanwhile, beat cream and remaining sugar in small bowl with electric mixer until soft peaks form; fold in mascarpone.
3 Dip biscuits, one at a time, in coffee mixture; place in single layer in shallow 2-litre (8-cup) serving dish. Pour any remaining coffee mixture over biscuits. Spread cream mixture over biscuits; sprinkle with combined chocolate and nuts.
4 Cover tiramisu; refrigerate 3 hours or overnight.

prep + cook time 20 minutes (+ refrigeration) **serves** 6
nutritional count per serving 40.5g total fat (22.2g saturated fat);
2153kJ (515 cal); 24.5g carbohydrate; 7g protein; 2g fibre

Zabaglione

2 eggs
4 egg yolks
½ cup (110g) caster (superfine) sugar
⅓ cup (80ml) marsala
12 sponge finger biscuits (140g)

1 Place eggs, yolks and sugar in large heatproof bowl over large saucepan of simmering water (make sure the water does not touch bottom of bowl).
2 With an electric hand mixer or whisk, beat egg mixture constantly until light and fluffy. With motor operating, gradually add marsala and continue beating about 10 minutes or until mixture is thick and creamy.
3 Spoon zabaglione into serving glasses; serve with biscuits.

prep + cook time 15 minutes **serves** 6
nutritional count per serving 6.6g total fat (2g saturated fat); 991kJ (237 cal); 34g carbohydrate; 6.2g protein; 0.3g fibre

Affogato with frangelico

⅓ cup ground espresso coffee beans
1½ cups (375ml) boiling water
1 litre (4 cups) vanilla ice-cream
½ cup (125ml) Frangelico

1 Place coffee and the water in coffee plunger; stand 4 minutes before plunging.
2 Place 2 scoops ice-cream in each of six small heatproof glasses or coffee cups; pour 1 tablespoon Frangelico over each. Pour over hot coffee; serve immediately.

prep time 10 minutes **serves** 6
nutritional count per serving 13.5g total fat (8.6g saturated fat); 1045kJ (250 cal); 23.2g carbohydrate; 3.9g protein; 0g fibre
tip While we used a hazelnut-flavoured liqueur in this recipe, you could use your favourite liqueur − orange and/or chocolate flavours also work well with coffee.

Nougat semifreddo
with orange honey syrup

1 vanilla bean
3 eggs, separated
⅓ cup (75g) caster (superfine) sugar
1½ cups (375ml) thickened (heavy) cream
200g (6½ ounces) nougat, chopped finely
½ cup (75g) coarsely chopped roasted shelled pistachios
1 tablespoon honey
orange honey syrup
¼ cup (90g) honey
1 tablespoon finely grated orange rind
2 tablespoons orange juice

1 Split vanilla bean in half lengthways; scrape seeds into small bowl, reserve pod for another use. Add yolks and sugar; beat with electric mixer until thick and creamy. Transfer mixture to large bowl.
2 Beat cream in small bowl with electric mixer until soft peaks form; gently fold cream into yolk mixture.
3 Beat egg whites in clean small bowl with electric mixer until soft peaks form. Gently fold half the egg whites into cream mixture; fold in nougat, nuts, honey and remaining egg white.
4 Spoon mixture into 14cm x 21cm (5½-inch x 8½-inch) loaf pan. Cover with foil; freeze 3 hours or until just firm.
5 Make orange honey syrup.
6 Stand semifreddo at room temperature 10 minutes before serving with syrup.
orange honey syrup Bring ingredients to the boil in small saucepan. Reduce heat; simmer, uncovered, 2 minutes.

prep + cook time 25 minutes (+ freezing) **serves** 4
nutritional count per serving 51.6g total fat (25.5g saturated fat); 3532kJ (845 cal); 87g carbohydrate; 13.3g protein; 2.2g fibre

Clove panna cotta with fresh figs

1 teaspoon whole cloves
1 ¼ cups (310ml) thickened (heavy) cream
⅔ cup (160ml) milk
2 teaspoons gelatine
2 tablespoons caster (superfine) sugar
½ teaspoon vanilla extract
2 tablespoons honey
4 medium fresh figs (240g)

1 Grease four ½-cup (125ml) moulds.
2 Place cloves, cream and milk in small saucepan; stand 10 minutes.
3 Sprinkle gelatine and sugar over cream mixture; stir over low heat, without boiling, until gelatine and sugar dissolve. Stir in extract. Strain mixture into medium jug; cool to room temperature.
4 Divide mixture among moulds. Cover; refrigerate 3 hours or until set.
5 Just before serving, stir honey in small saucepan until warm. Cut figs into quarters.
6 Turn panna cotta onto serving plates; top with figs and drizzle with warm honey.

prep + cook time 30 minutes (+ cooling & refrigeration) **serves** 4
nutritional count per serving 29.3g total fat (19.2g saturated fat); 1639kJ (392 cal); 29.1g carbohydrate; 5.1g protein; 1.3g fibre
tip You can use a 300ml carton of cream without affecting the recipe.

Italian ricotta cheesecake

90g (3 ounces) butter, softened
¼ cup (55g) caster (superfine) sugar
1 egg
1¼ cups (185g) plain (all-purpose) flour
¼ cup (35g) self-raising flour
filling
1kg (2 pounds) ricotta cheese
1 tablespoon finely grated lemon rind
¼ cup (60ml) lemon juice
1 cup (220g) caster (superfine) sugar
5 eggs
¼ cup (40g) sultanas
¼ cup (80g) finely chopped glacé fruit salad

1 Beat butter, sugar and egg in small bowl with electric mixer until combined. Stir in half the sifted flours; then work in remaining flour with your hand. Knead pastry on floured surface until smooth; wrap in plastic; refrigerate 30 minutes.
2 Grease 28cm (11¼-inch) springform tin. Press pastry over base of tin; prick with fork. Place on oven tray; refrigerate another 30 minutes.
3 Preheat oven to 200°C/400°F.
4 Line pastry with baking paper, fill with dried beans or rice; bake 10 minutes. Remove paper and beans; bake further 15 minutes or until browned lightly. Cool.
5 Reduce oven to 160°C/325°F.
6 Make filling by processing cheese, rind, juice, sugar and eggs until smooth. Stir in sultanas and glacé fruit. Pour filling into tin.
7 Bake cheesecake about 50 minutes. Cool in oven with door ajar. Refrigerate cheesecake 3 hours or overnight. Serve dusted with sifted icing sugar, if you like.

prep + cook time 1 hour 35 minutes (+ refrigeration) **serves** 16
nutritional count per serving 13.8g total fat (8.2g saturated fat);
1262kJ (302 cal); 33.2g carbohydrate; 10.7g protein; 0.7g fibre

Balsamic strawberries with mascarpone

500g (1 pound) strawberries, halved
¼ cup (55g) caster (superfine) sugar
2 tablespoons balsamic vinegar
1 cup (250g) mascarpone cheese
1 tablespoon icing (confectioner's) sugar
1 teaspoon vanilla extract
¼ cup coarsely chopped fresh mint

1 Combine strawberries, sugar and vinegar in medium bowl.
Cover; refrigerate 20 minutes.
2 Meanwhile, combine mascarpone, icing sugar and extract in
small bowl.
3 Stir mint into strawberry mixture; divide among serving dishes.
Serve with mascarpone mixture.

prep time 10 minutes (+ refrigeration) **serves** 4
nutritional count per serving 29.8g total fat (20.3g saturated fat);
1572kJ (376 cal); 21.2g carbohydrate; 5.2g protein; 3g fibre

Walnut and ricotta-stuffed figs

8 medium figs (480g)
¼ cup (25g) roasted walnuts, chopped coarsely
½ cup (120g) ricotta cheese
1 tablespoon caster (superfine) sugar
⅓ cup (80ml) pouring cream
30g (1 ounce) butter
⅓ cup (75g) firmly packed light brown sugar

1 Preheat oven to 200°C/400°F.
2 Cut figs, from the top, into quarters, being careful not to cut all the way through; open slightly. Place on oven tray.
3 Combine nuts, cheese and caster sugar in small bowl; divide mixture among figs.
4 Bake figs about 10 minutes or until figs are heated through.
5 Meanwhile, stir cream, butter and brown sugar in small saucepan over heat until sugar dissolves; simmer, uncovered, 3 minutes.
6 Place two figs in each serving dish; drizzle with caramel sauce.

prep + cook time 20 minutes **serves** 4
nutritional count per serving 22.8g total fat (12.2g saturated fat); 1526kJ (365 cal); 32.6g carbohydrate; 6g protein; 3.1g fibre

Mixed berry and mascarpone bruschetta

1¼ cups (310ml) thickened (heavy) cream
1 tablespoon icing (confectioner's) sugar
250g (8 ounces) mascarpone cheese
6 thick slices brioche (200g)
150g (5 ounces) raspberries
150g (5 ounces) blueberries

1 Beat cream and sugar in small bowl with electric mixer until soft peaks form; fold in mascarpone.
2 Preheat grill (broiler).
3 Place brioche slices under grill until lightly toasted both sides.
4 Serve brioche topped with mascarpone mixture and berries.

prep + cook time 15 minutes **serves** 6
nutritional count per serving 47.6g total fat (29.8g saturated fat); 2725kJ (652 cal); 46.4g carbohydrate; 9.9g protein; 3.3g fibre
tip You can use a 300ml carton of cream without affecting the recipe.

Muscat granita with figs and honey fennel syrup

1 cup (250ml) water
½ cup (125ml) muscat
½ cup (110g) caster (superfine) sugar
1 teaspoon black peppercorns
1 teaspoon finely grated lemon rind
1 tablespoon lemon juice
1 tablespoon fennel seeds
½ cup (125ml) water, extra
¼ cup (90g) honey
8 large fresh figs (640g)

1 Bring the water, muscat, sugar, peppercorns, rind and juice to the boil in small saucepan. Cool 10 minutes.
2 Strain muscat mixture into 14cm x 21cm (5½-inch x 8½-inch) loaf pan. Cover with foil; freeze about 4 hours or until firm, scraping granita from bottom and sides of pan with fork every hour.
3 Dry-fry fennel seeds in small saucepan until fragrant. Add the extra water and honey; bring to the boil. Reduce heat; simmer, uncovered, without stirring, about 5 minutes or until mixture thickens slightly. Strain through sieve into small jug; discard seeds. Cool syrup 10 minutes.
4 Cut figs lengthways into five slices; divide among serving plates. Drizzle figs with syrup; top with granita.

prep + cook time 25 minutes (+ freezing) **serves** 4
nutritional count per serving 0.5g total fat (0g saturated fat); 1216kJ (291 cal); 62.9g carbohydrate; 2.4g protein; 4g fibre

Ricotta and mascarpone tarts with roasted pears

1 ½ cups (225g) plain
   (all-purpose) flour
½ cup (80g) icing (confectioner's)
   sugar
125g (4 ounces) butter, chopped
1 egg
filling
1 ¼ cups (250g) ricotta cheese
½ cup (110g) caster
   (superfine) sugar

½ cup (125g) mascarpone cheese
2 eggs
2 teaspoons finely grated
   lemon rind
roasted pears
8 small pears (1kg), peeled,
   quartered, cored
1 tablespoon lemon juice
⅓ cup (75g) caster
   (superfine) sugar

1 Preheat oven to 180°C/350°F. Grease eight 8cm (3¼-inch) round fluted flan tins.

2 Process flour, sugar and butter until crumbly. Add egg; process until ingredients just come together. Knead dough on floured surface 30 seconds or until smooth. Cover; refrigerate 30 minutes.

3 Divide pastry into eight portions. Roll each portion between sheets baking paper until large enough to line tins. Line tins with pastry; trim edges. Place on oven tray. Line pastry with baking paper; fill with dried beans or rice. Bake 15 minutes. Remove paper and beans; bake further 15 minutes or until pastry is browned lightly. Cool 10 minutes.

4 Reduce oven to 150°C/300°F.

5 Make filling by beating ricotta and sugar in small bowl with electric mixer 2 minutes or until smooth. Beat in mascarpone, eggs and rind until just combined. Pour filling into pastry cases.

6 Bake tarts about 25 minutes or until just set. Cool to room temperature.

7 Increase oven to 240°C/475°F; make roasted pears.

8 Top tarts with cooled pears.

roasted pears Line baking dish with baking paper. Place pears in dish; sprinkle with juice and sugar. Bake, turning occasionally, 15 minutes or until browned and tender.

prep + cook time 1 hour 50 minutes (+ refrigeration) **serves** 4
nutritional count per serving 52.3g total fat (32.9g saturated fat); 4477kJ (1071 cal); 127.4g carbohydrate; 19.9g protein; 5.7g fibre

Pistachio and polenta cake with blood orange syrup

1¼ cups (300g) sour cream
125g (4 ounces) butter, softened
1 cup (220g) caster (superfine) sugar
2 cups (300g) self-raising flour
½ teaspoon bicarbonate of soda
⅔ cup (110g) polenta
1 teaspoon finely grated blood orange rind
¾ cup (180ml) water
⅔ cup (100g) roasted shelled pistachios
blood orange syrup
1 cup (250ml) blood orange juice
1 cup (220g) caster (superfine) sugar
1 cinnamon stick

1 Preheat oven to 160°C/325°F. Grease deep 20cm (8-inch) round cake pan; line base and side with baking paper.
2 Make blood orange syrup.
3 Beat sour cream, butter, sugar, sifted flour and soda, polenta, rind and the water in large bowl with electric mixer on low speed until just combined. Beat on medium speed until mixture changes to a slightly lighter colour; stir in nuts. Spread mixture into pan.
4 Bake cake about 1 hour. Stand cake in pan 10 minutes; turn cake, top-side up, onto wire rack to cool.
5 Serve cake warm or cold with strained blood orange syrup.
blood orange syrup Bring ingredients to the boil, stirring, in small saucepan. Reduce heat; simmer, uncovered, about 15 minutes or until syrup thickens. Cool to room temperature.

prep + cook time 1 hour 25 minutes **serves** 12
nutritional count per serving 15.2g total fat (7.6g saturated fat); 1714kJ (412 cal); 64.3g carbohydrate; 5.6g protein; 2.1g fibre

Dark chocolate and hazelnut parfait

½ cup (125ml) thickened (heavy) cream
½ cup (165g) chocolate hazelnut spread
¼ cup (60ml) coffee-flavoured liqueur
2 eggs
3 egg yolks
⅓ cup (75g) caster (superfine) sugar
1 cup (250ml) thickened (heavy) cream, extra
155g (5 ounces) dark eating chocolate, grated coarsely
⅓ cup (40g) finely chopped roasted hazelnuts
90g (3 ounces) dark eating chocolate, grated coarsely, extra

1 Line six-hole (¾-cup/180ml) texas muffin pan with paper cases.
2 Stir cream, chocolate hazelnut spread and liqueur in small saucepan over low heat until smooth.
3 Beat eggs, egg yolks and sugar in small bowl with electric mixer until thick and creamy; with motor operating, gradually beat warm chocolate mixture into egg mixture. Transfer parfait mixture to large bowl; refrigerate 20 minutes or until mixture thickens slightly.
4 Beat extra cream in small bowl with electric mixer until soft peaks form; fold into parfait mixture with grated chocolate and nuts. Pour mixture into cases. Cover loosely with plastic wrap; freeze overnight.
5 Lift parfaits out of pan; serve immediately, topped with extra grated chocolate.

prep + cook time 30 minutes (+ refrigeration & freezing) **makes** 6
nutritional count per parfait 52.4g total fat (26.4g saturated fat);
3231kJ (773 cal); 61.2g carbohydrate; 9.9g protein; 1.5g fibre

Chocolate hazelnut gelato

1 cup (125g) hazelnuts
1⅔ cups (400ml) milk
2½ cups (625ml) pouring cream
6 egg yolks
⅓ cup (75g) caster (superfine) sugar
¾ cup (215g) chocolate hazelnut spread

1 Preheat oven to 180°C/350°F.
2 Roast hazelnuts in a shallow baking dish about 8 minutes or until skins begin to split and nuts are toasted. Place nuts in clean tea towel and rub vigorously to remove skins. Chop nuts coarsely.
3 Bring milk, cream and hazelnuts to the boil in medium saucepan; cover, remove from heat. Stand 10 minutes; strain, discard hazelnuts.
4 Whisk egg yolks and sugar in medium bowl until creamy. Gradually whisk hot milk mixture into egg mixture. Return to saucepan, stir over low heat, without boiling, until mixture thickens slightly and coats back of spoon. Whisk in chocolate hazelnut spread until combined.
5 Transfer custard mixture to large bowl, cover surface with plastic wrap; cool slightly. Refrigerate 2 hours or until cold.
6 Transfer mixture to shallow container, cover with foil and freeze until almost firm. Chop gelato coarsely; blend or process until smooth. Pour into deep dish or container; cover, freeze until firm.

prep + cook time 40 minutes (+ refrigeration & freezing) **serves** 8
nutritional count per serving 57.1g total fat (27.2g saturated fat); 2796kJ (669 cal); 30.2g carbohydrate; 9.5g protein; 1.9g fibre
tip You can use a 600ml carton of cream without affecting the recipe.

Cassata

2 eggs, separated
½ cup (80g) icing
   (confectioner's) sugar
½ cup (125ml) pouring cream
few drops almond essence
chocolate layer
2 eggs, separated
½ cup (80g) icing
   (confectioner's) sugar
½ cup (125ml) pouring cream
60g (2 ounces) dark eating
   chocolate, melted
2 tablespoons cocoa powder
1½ tablespoons water

fruit layer
1 cup (250ml) pouring cream
1 teaspoon vanilla extract
1 egg white, beaten lightly
⅓ cup (55g) icing
   (confectioner's) sugar
2 tablespoons red glacé cherries,
   chopped finely
2 glacé apricots, chopped finely
2 glacé pineapple rings,
   chopped finely
1 tablespoon green glacé cherries,
   chopped finely
30g (1 ounce) flaked almonds,
   roasted

1 Beat egg whites in small bowl with electric mixer until firm peaks form; gradually beat in sifted sugar. Fold in lightly beaten egg yolks.
2 Beat cream and essence in small bowl with electric mixer until soft peaks form; fold into egg mixture. Pour mixture into deep 20cm (8-inch) round cake pan. Level top; freeze until firm.
3 Make chocolate layer; spread over almond layer. Freeze until firm.
4 Make fruit layer; spread over chocolate layer. Freeze until firm.
5 Run small spatula around edge of cassata; wipe hot cloth over base and side of pan. Turn cassata onto serving plate.
chocolate layer Beat egg whites in small bowl with electric mixer until firm peaks form; gradually beat in sifted sugar. Beat cream in small bowl until soft peaks form; fold into egg white mixture. Combine chocolate and egg yolks in small bowl; stir in blended cocoa and water. Fold chocolate mixture through cream mixture.
fruit layer Beat cream and extract in small bowl with electric mixer until firm peaks form. Beat egg white in small bowl with electric mixer until soft peaks form; gradually add sifted sugar. Fold egg white mixture into cream; fold in fruit and nuts.

prep time 1 hour (+ freezing) **serves** 8
nutritional count per serving 34.4g total fat (20.4g saturated fat); 2307kJ (552 cal); 57.8g carbohydrate; 6.6g protein; 0.7g fibre

Grapefruit sorbetto

2 tablespoons finely grated ruby grapefruit rind
1 cup (220g) caster (superfine) sugar
2½ cups (625ml) water
¾ cup (180ml) ruby red grapefruit juice
1 egg white

1 Stir rind, sugar and the water in medium saucepan over high heat until sugar dissolves; bring to the boil. Reduce heat; simmer, without stirring, uncovered, 5 minutes. Transfer to large heatproof jug, cool to room temperature. Stir in juice.
2 Pour sorbet mixture into loaf pan; cover tightly with foil. Freeze 3 hours or overnight.
3 Process sorbet mixture with egg white until smooth. Return to loaf pan. Cover; freeze until firm. Serve with extra grapefruit rind, if you like.

prep + cook time 30 minutes (+ cooling & freezing) **serves** 8
nutritional count per serving 0g total fat (0g saturated fat); 481kJ (115 cal); 29.3g carbohydrate; 0.6g protein; 0.1g fibre

glossary

almonds
flaked paper-thin slices.
ground also called almond meal.
slivered small pieces cut lengthways.
artichokes
globe large flower-bud of a member of the thistle family; it has tough petal-like leaves, and is edible in part when cooked.
hearts tender centre of the globe artichoke; is obtained after the choke is removed. Cooked hearts are available in brine or marinated in oil.
bacon slices also called bacon rashers.
baking powder a raising agent consisting of two parts cream of tartar to one part bicarbonate of soda (baking soda).
basil, sweet the most common type of basil.
bay leaves aromatic leaves from the bay tree available fresh or dried; adds a strong, slightly peppery flavour.
beans
borlotti also called roman or pink beans; pale pink/beige with dark red streaks, they are eaten fresh or dried.
broad also called fava, windsor and horse beans; available dried, fresh, canned and frozen. Fresh should be peeled twice

(discard outer green pod and beige-green inner shell); the frozen beans have had their pods removed but the beige shell still needs removal.
cannellini small white bean similar to other *phaseolus vulgaris* varieties (great northern, navy or haricot). Available dried or canned.
white a generic term we use for canned or dried cannellini, haricot, navy or great northern beans.
beef, eye fillet tenderloin, fillet; fine texture, most expensive and extremely tender.
beetroot also called red beets; firm, round root vegetable.
bicarbonate of soda also called baking soda.
blood orange a virtually seedless citrus fruit with blood-red-streaked rind and flesh; sweet, non-acidic, salmon-coloured pulp and juice with slight strawberry or raspberry overtones. The rind is not as bitter as an ordinary orange.
breadcrumbs
packaged prepared fine-textured but crunchy white breadcrumbs; good for coating foods that are to be fried.
stale crumbs made by grating, blending or processing 1- or 2-day-old bread.

brioche French in origin; a rich, yeast-leavened, cake-like bread made with butter and eggs. Available from cake or specialty bread shops.
butter we use salted butter unless stated.
buttermilk originally the term for the slightly sour liquid left after butter was churned from cream, today it is made like yogurt. Sold with milk products in supermarkets. Despite the implication, it is low in fat.
capers grey-green buds of a warm climate shrub, sold dried and salted or pickled in a vinegar brine; tiny young ones (baby capers) are available in brine or dried in salt.
capsicum also called pepper or bell pepper.
cheese
blue mould-treated cheeses mottled with blue veining. Varieties include firm and crumbly stilton types and mild, creamy brie-like cheeses.
bocconcini from the diminutive of "boccone", meaning mouthful in Italian; walnut-sized, baby mozzarella, a delicate, semi-soft, white cheese. Sold fresh, it spoils rapidly; refrigerate in brine for 1 or 2 days.
fetta Greek in origin; a crumbly textured goat's- or sheep's-milk cheese with a sharp, salty taste.

fontina an Italian cow's-milk cheese with a smooth but firm texture and a mild, nutty flavour. Use mozzarella or taleggio as a substitute.

goat's made from goat's milk; has an earthy, strong taste. Available soft, crumbly and firm, in various shapes and sizes, and sometimes rolled in ash or herbs.

gorgonzola a creamy Italian blue cheese with a mild, sweet taste; good as an accompaniment to fruit or used to flavour sauces (such as pasta).

gruyère a hard-rind swiss cheese with small holes and a nutty, slightly salty flavour.

haloumi a Greek Cypriot cheese with a semi-firm, spongy texture and salty sweet flavour. Ripened and stored in salted whey; best grilled or fried, and holds its shape well on being heated. Eat while still warm as it becomes tough and rubbery on cooling.

mascarpone an Italian fresh cultured-cream product made similarly to yogurt. Whiteish to creamy yellow in colour, with a buttery-rich, luscious texture. Is soft, creamy and spreadable.

mozzarella soft, spun-curd cheese; traditionally made from water-buffalo milk. Now generally made from cow's milk, it is the most popular pizza cheese because of its low melting point and elasticity when heated.

parmesan also called parmigiano; a hard, grainy cow's-milk cheese originating in the Parma region of Italy. The curd is salted in brine for a month then aged for up to 2 years.

pizza cheese a commercial blend of grated mozzarella, cheddar and parmesan.

provolone a mild stretched-curd cheese similar to mozzarella when young, becoming hard, spicy and grainy the longer it's aged. Golden yellow in colour, with a smooth waxy rind, provolone is a good all-purpose cheese.

ricotta soft, sweet, moist, white cow's-milk cheese with a low fat content (8.5 per cent) and a slightly grainy texture. Its name roughly translates as "cooked again" and refers to ricotta's manufacture from a whey that is itself a by-product of other cheese making.

chicken

breast fillet breast halved, skinned, boned.

drumsticks leg with skin and bone intact.

small chicken also called spatchcock or poussin; no more than 6 weeks old, weighing a maximum of 500g. Spatchcock is also a cooking term to describe splitting poultry open, flattening and grilling.

tenderloins thin strip of meat lying just under the breast.

chickpeas also called garbanzos, hummus or channa; an irregularly round, sandy-coloured legume. Available canned or dried (needs several hours soaking in cold water before use).

chilli use rubber gloves when handling fresh chillies as they can burn your skin. We use unseeded chillies as the seeds contain the heat.

flakes also sold as crushed chilli; dehydrated deep-red extremely fine slices and whole seeds.

thai also called "scuds"; tiny, very hot and bright red in colour.

chocolate

dark eating also called semi-sweet or luxury chocolate; contains a high percentage of cocoa liquor and cocoa butter, and little added sugar. Unless stated otherwise, we use dark eating chocolate in this book as it's ideal for use in desserts and cakes.

white eating contains no cocoa solids but derives its sweet flavour from cocoa butter. Very sensitive to heat.

chocolate hazelnut spread also known as Nutella; made of cocoa powder, hazelnuts, sugar and milk.

ciabatta meaning 'slipper' in Italian, the traditional shape of this popular crisp-crusted, open-textured white sourdough bread.

cinnamon available in pieces (sticks or quills) and ground into powder.

cloves dried flower buds of a tropical tree; used whole or ground. They have a strong scent and taste so use sparingly.

cocoa powder also known as unsweetened cocoa.

cornflour also called cornstarch. Made from corn or wheat.

cranberries available dried and frozen; have a rich, astringent flavour and can be used in cooking sweet and savoury dishes. The dried version can usually be substituted for or with other dried fruit.

cream we use fresh pouring cream, also known as pure cream. It has no additives, and contains a minimum fat content of 35 per cent.

thickened a whipping cream that contains a thickener (minimum fat content of 35 per cent).

crème fraîche a mature, naturally fermented cream (minimum 35 per cent fat) with a velvety texture and slightly tangy, nutty flavour. This French sour cream can boil without curdling; use in sweet and savoury dishes.

cumin also called zeera or comino; resembling caraway in size, cumin is the dried seed of a parsley-related plant with a spicy, almost curry-like flavour. Available dried as seeds or ground.

eggs we use large (60g) chicken eggs unless stated otherwise. If a recipe calls for raw or barely cooked eggs, exercise caution if there is a salmonella problem in your area, particularly in food eaten by children and pregnant women.

dill also called dill weed; used fresh or dried, in seed form or ground. Its feathery, frond-like fresh leaves are grassier and more subtle than the dried version or the seeds.

eggplant also called aubergine. Ranging in size from tiny to very large and in colour from pale green to deep purple. Can also be purchased char-grilled, packed in oil, in jars.

fennel also called finocchio or anise; a crunchy green vegetable slightly resembling celery. Dried fennel seeds are also available; they have a stronger licorice flavour.

figs are best eaten in peak season, at the height of summer. Vary in skin and flesh colour according to type not ripeness. When ripe, figs should be unblemished and bursting with flesh.

flour

plain unbleached wheat flour is the best for baking: the gluten content ensures a strong dough, which produces a light result.

self-raising plain or wholemeal flour with baking powder and salt added; make at home in the proportion of 1 cup flour to 2 teaspoons baking powder.

gelatine we use dried (powdered) gelatine; it's also available in sheet form called leaf gelatine. Three teaspoons of dried gelatine (8g or one sachet) is about the same as four sheets.

glacé fruit fruit such as pineapple, apricots, peaches and pears that are cooked in a heavy sugar syrup then dried.

hazelnuts also called filberts; plump, grape-sized, rich, sweet nut with a brown skin. Remove skin by rubbing heated nuts together vigorously in a tea-towel.

honey honey sold in a squeezable container is not suitable for the recipes in this book.

lentils dried pulses often identified by and named after their colour (red, brown, yellow).

marsala a fortified Italian wine produced in the region surrounding the Sicilian city of Marsala; recognisable by its intense amber colour and complex aroma. Often used in cooking.

mayonnaise we use whole-egg mayonnaise; a commercial product of high quality made with whole eggs and labelled as such.

milk we use full-cream homogenised milk unless stated otherwise.

mushrooms

button small, cultivated white mushrooms with a mild flavour. When a recipe in this book calls for an unspecified mushroom, use button.

chanterelle also called girolles or pfifferling; a trumpet-shaped wild mushroom, ranging in colour from yellow to orange, with a delicate flavour and chewy texture. Also available dried.

chestnut are cultivated mushrooms with a firm texture and strong flavour. They are available only irregularly.

flat large and flat with a rich earthy flavour. Sometimes misnamed field mushrooms which are wild mushrooms.

oyster also called abalone; grey-white and shaped like a fan. Prized for its smooth texture and subtle, oyster-like flavour. Also available pink.

porcini, dried also called cèpes; the richest-flavoured mushrooms. Expensive, but because they're so strongly flavoured, only a small amount is required.

shiitake fresh, are also called chinese black, forest or golden oak mushrooms. Although cultivated, they have the earthiness and taste of wild mushrooms. They are large and meaty.

swiss brown also called roman or cremini. Light to dark brown mushrooms with full-bodied flavour.

mustard

dijon also called french. Pale brown, creamy, distinctively flavoured, fairly mild french mustard.

wholegrain also called seeded. A French-style coarse-grain mustard made from crushed mustard seeds and dijon-style french mustard.

oil

cooking spray we use a cholesterol-free spray made from canola oil.

olive made from ripened olives. Extra virgin and virgin are the first and second press, respectively, of the

olives and are therefore considered the best; the "extra light" or "light" on other types refers to taste not fat levels.

vegetable any number of oils from plant rather than animal fats.

onion

green also called scallion or (incorrectly) shallot; an immature onion picked before the bulb has formed, having a long, bright-green edible stalk.

red also called spanish, red spanish or bermuda onion; a sweet-flavoured, large, purple-red onion.

spring crisp, narrow green-leafed tops and a round sweet white bulb; larger than green onions.

oregano also called wild marjoram; has a woody stalk and clumps of tiny, dark-green leaves. Has a pungent, peppery flavour.

pancetta an Italian unsmoked bacon.

paprika ground dried, sweet red capsicum (bell pepper); varieties available include sweet, hot, mild and smoked.

pasta

farfalle bow-tie shaped short pasta; sometimes called butterfly pasta.

fettuccine fresh or dried ribbon pasta made from durum wheat, semolina and egg. Also available plain or flavoured.

389

fusilli "little spindles", also called corkscrews; are a dried spiral pasta.

orecchiette Italian for "little ears"; named after their shape, resembling tiny human ears.

penne Italian for "pen", named after their shape, resembling a quill, and has angled ends and ridges; also available in a smooth variety.

ravioli "little turnips", squares of pasta stuffed with cheese, vegetables or meat. Usually made from fresh pasta either by hand or in moulds.

rigatoni Italian for "large, ridged", this dried ribbed, tubular pasta is perfect with any sauce and is also good for pasta bakes.

pepitas the pale green kernels of dried pumpkin seeds; they can be bought plain or salted.

polenta also known as cornmeal; a flour-like cereal made of dried corn (maize). Also the dish made from it.

prosciutto unsmoked Italian ham; salted, air-cured and aged, it is usually eaten uncooked.

quail related to the pheasant and partridge; a small, delicate-flavoured farmed game bird ranging in weight from 250g to 300g.

radicchio Italian in origin; a member of the chicory family. The dark burgundy leaves and strong, bitter flavour can be cooked or eaten raw in salads.

rice, arborio small, round grain rice well-suited to absorb a large amount of liquid; the high level of starch makes it suitable for risottos, giving the dish its classic creaminess.

roasting/toasting nuts and dried coconut can be roasted in the oven to restore their fresh flavour and release aromatic oils; spread evenly onto an oven tray, roast in a moderate oven about 5 minutes. Desiccated coconut, pine nuts and sesame seeds roast more evenly if stirred over low heat in a heavy-based frying pan; their natural oils help turn them golden.

rocket also called arugula and rucola; peppery green leaf eaten raw or used in cooking. Baby rocket leaves are smaller and less peppery.

saffron stigma of a member of the crocus family, available ground or in strands; imparts a yellow-orange colour once infused. The quality varies greatly; the best is the most expensive spice in the world.

sashimi fish sold as sashimi has to meet stringent guidelines regarding handling. Seek advice from local authorities before eating any raw seafood.

savoy cabbage large, heavy head with crinkled dark-green outer leaves; a fairly mild cabbage.

seafood

marinara mix a mixture of uncooked, chopped seafood available from fishmarkets and fishmongers.

mussels should only be bought from a reliable fish market: they must be tightly closed when bought, indicating they are alive. Before cooking, scrub shells with a strong brush to remove beards; do not eat any that do not open after cooking.

octopus usually tenderised before you buy them; both octopus and squid require either long slow cooking (for large molluscs) or quick cooking over high heat (for small molluscs) – anything in between will make the octopus tough and rubbery.

squid also called calamari; a type of mollusc. Buy squid hoods to make preparation and cooking faster.

swordfish also called broadbill. Substitute with yellowfin or bluefin tuna or mahi mahi.

semolina coarsely ground flour milled from durum wheat.

shallots also called french shallots, golden shallots or eschalots. Small and elongated, with a brown-skin, they grow in tight clusters similar to garlic.

silver beet also called swiss chard and incorrectly, spinach; has fleshy stalks and large leaves.

sopressa a salami from the north of Italy; available mild and chilli-flavoured. If you can't find it easily, use any hot salami – the taste won't be exactly the same.

spinach also called english spinach and incorrectly, silver beet. Baby spinach leaves are best eaten raw in salads; the larger leaves should be added last to soups, stews and stir-fries, and should be cooked until barely wilted.

sponge finger biscuits also called savoiardi, savoy biscuits or lady's fingers, they are Italian-style crisp fingers made from sponge cake mixture.

sugar

brown a soft, finely granulated sugar retaining molasses for colour and flavour.

caster also called superfine or finely granulated table sugar.

icing also known as confectioners' sugar or powdered sugar; pulverised granulated sugar crushed together with a small amount of cornflour.

pure icing also known as confectioners' sugar or powdered sugar.

tomato

bottled pasta sauce a prepared sauce; often a blend of tomatoes, herbs and spices.

canned whole peeled tomatoes in natural juices; available crushed, chopped or diced. Use undrained.

cherry also called tiny tim or tom thumb; small and round.

egg also called plum or roma; smallish, oval-shaped tomatoes.

paste triple-concentrated tomato puree used to flavour soups, stews, sauces and casseroles.

puree canned pureed tomatoes (not tomato paste); substitute with fresh peeled and pureed tomatoes.

semi-dried partially dried tomato pieces in olive oil; softer and juicier than sun-dried, these are not preserved so do not keep as long as sun-dried.

sun-dried tomato pieces dried with salt; this dehydrates the tomato, concentrating the flavour. We use sun-dried tomatoes in oil, unless stated otherwise.

vanilla

bean dried, long, thin pod; the minuscule black seeds inside are used to impart a vanilla flavour.

extract obtained from vanilla beans infused in water; a non-alcoholic version of essence.

veal, osso buco also called veal shin, usually cut into 3cm to 5cm thick slices and used in the famous Italian slow-cooked casserole of the same name.

vinegar

balsamic originally from Modena, Italy, there are now many on the market ranging in pungency and quality depending on how, and for how long, they have been aged. Quality can be determined up to a point by price; use the most expensive sparingly.

cider made from fermented apples.

witlof also called belgian endive; related to and confused with chicory. A versatile vegetable, it tastes good cooked and raw.

yeast (dried and fresh), a raising agent. Granular (7g sachets) and fresh (20g blocks) yeast can almost always be used interchangeably.

zucchini also called courgette; harvested when young, its edible flowers can be stuffed and deep-fried.

index

conversion chart

MEASURES

One Australian metric measuring cup holds approximately 250ml, one Australian metric tablespoon holds 20ml, one Australian metric teaspoon holds 5ml.

The difference between one country's measuring cups and another's is within a two- or three-teaspoon variance, and will not affect your cooking results. North America, New Zealand and the United Kingdom use a 15ml tablespoon.

All cup and spoon measurements are level. The most accurate way of measuring dry ingredients is to weigh them. When measuring liquids, use a clear glass or plastic jug with the metric markings.

We use large eggs with an average weight of 60g.

LIQUID MEASURES

METRIC	IMPERIAL
30ml	1 fluid oz
60ml	2 fluid oz
100ml	3 fluid oz
125ml	4 fluid oz
150ml	5 fluid oz (¼ pint/1 gill)
190ml	6 fluid oz
250ml	8 fluid oz
300ml	10 fluid oz (½ pint)
500ml	16 fluid oz
600ml	20 fluid oz (1 pint)
1000ml (1 litre)	1¾ pints

LENGTH MEASURES

METRIC	IMPERIAL
3mm	⅛in
6mm	¼in
1cm	½in
2cm	¾in
2.5cm	1in
5cm	2in
6cm	2½in
8cm	3in
10cm	4in
13cm	5in
15cm	6in
18cm	7in
20cm	8in
23cm	9in
25cm	10in
28cm	11in
30cm	12in (1ft)

DRY MEASURES

METRIC	IMPERIAL
15g	½oz
30g	1oz
60g	2oz
90g	3oz
125g	4oz (¼lb)
155g	5oz
185g	6oz
220g	7oz
250g	8oz (½lb)
280g	9oz
315g	10oz
345g	11oz
375g	12oz (¾lb)
410g	13oz
440g	14oz
470g	15oz
500g	16oz (1lb)
750g	24oz (1½lb)
1kg	32oz (2lb)

OVEN TEMPERATURES

The oven temperatures in this book are for conventional ovens; if you have a fan-forced oven, decrease the temperature by 10-20 degrees.

	°C (CELSIUS)	°F (FAHRENHEIT)
Very slow	120	250
Slow	150	300
Moderately slow	160	325
Moderate	180	350
Moderately hot	200	400
Hot	220	425
Very hot	240	475

Published in 2010 by ACP Books, Sydney
ACP Books are published by ACP Magazines,
a division of PBL Media Pty Limited

ACP BOOKS

General manager Christine Whiston
Editor-in-chief Susan Tomnay
Creative director & designer Hieu Chi Nguyen
Art director Hannah Blackmore
Senior editor Stephanie Kistner
Food director Pamela Clark
Food editor Cathie Lonnie
Sales & rights director Brian Cearnes
Marketing manager Bridget Cody
Senior business analyst Rebecca Varela
Operations manager David Scotto
Production manager Victoria Jefferys

Published by ACP Books, a division of ACP Magazines Ltd.
54 Park St, Sydney NSW Australia 2000. GPO Box 4088, Sydney, NSW 2001.
Phone +61 2 9282 8618 Fax +61 2 9267 9438
acpbooks@acpmagazines.com.au www.acpbooks.com.au

Printed by Toppan Printing Co., China.

Australia Distributed by Network Services, GPO Box 4088, Sydney, NSW 2001.
Phone +61 2 9282 8777 Fax +61 2 9264 3278
networkweb@networkservicescompany.com.au
New Zealand Distributed by Southern Publishers Group, 21 Newton Road, Auckland.
Phone +64 9 360 0692 Fax +64 9 360 0695 hub@spg.co.nz
South Africa Distributed by PSD Promotions, 30 Diesel Road Isando, Gauteng Johannesburg.
PO Box 1175, Isando 1600, Gauteng Johannesburg.
Phone +27 11 392 6065/6/7 Fax +27 11 392 6079/80 orders@psdprom.co.za

Title: Italian / food director Pamela Clark
ISBN: 978-1-74245-022-3 (pbk)
Notes: Includes index.
Subjects: Cookery, Italian.
Other authors/contributors: Clark, Pamela
Dewey number: 641.5945
© ACP Magazines Ltd 2010
ABN 18 053 273 546
This publication is copyright. No part of it may be reproduced or
transmitted in any form without the written permission of the publishers.

To order books, phone 136 116 (within Australia) or
order online at www.acpbooks.com.au
Send recipe enquiries to: recipeenquiries@acpmagazines.com.au

Front cover & additional photography Vanessa Levis
Front cover & additional styling Matt Page
Front cover & additional food preparation Elizabeth Macri